BETWEEN

THE EAGLE

AND

THE SUN

Also by Ihab Hassan

Radical Innocence: Studies in the
Contemporary American Novel (1961)

The Literature of Silence:
Henry Miller and Samuel Beckett (1967)

The Dismemberment of Orpheus:
Toward a Postmodern Literature (1971, 1982)

Liberations: New Essays on the
Humanities in Revolution (editor) (1972)

Contemporary American Literature, 1945–1972 (1973)

Paracriticisms: Seven Speculations of the Times (1975)

The Right Promethean Fire:
Imagination, Science, and Cultural Change (1980)

Innovation/Renovation: New Perspectives on the Humanities
(edited with Sally Hassan) (1983)

Out of Egypt: Fragments of an Autobiography (1986)

The Postmodern Turn:
Essays in Postmodern Theory and Culture (1987)

Selves at Risk: Patterns of Quest
in Contemporary American Letters (1990)

Rumors of Change: Essays of Five Decades (1995)

BETWEEN

THE EAGLE

AND

THE SUN

Traces of Japan

IHAB HASSAN

The University of Alabama Press   *Tuscaloosa and London*

∞

The paper on which this book is printed meets the minimum re-
quirements of American National Standard for Information Science-
Permanence of Paper for Printed Library Materials, ANSI Z39.48-
1984.

Library of Congress Cataloging-in-Publication Data

Hassan, Ihab Habib, 1925—
Between the Eagle and the Sun : traces of Japan / Ihab Hassan.
p.   cm.
ISBN 0-8173-0819-9 (alk. paper)
1. Japan—Civilization.   2. East and West.   3. Americans—
Japan—Biography.   4. Japan—Ethnic relations.   I. Title.
DS821.H3497   1996
952.04—dc20   95-13544
                                                        CIP

British Library Cataloguing-in-Publication Data available

S

For Iwao Iwamoto and Donald Richie

In this mortal frame of mine which is made of a hundred bones and nine orifices there is something, and this something is called a wind-swept spirit for lack of a better name, for it is much like a thin drapery that is torn and swept away at the slightest stir of the wind.

—Matsuo Basho, *The Narrow Road to the Deep North*

But it seems to me that this egotism of a traveller, however incessant—however shameless and obtrusive, must still convey some true ideas of the country through which he has passed. His very selfishness . . . compels him, as it were, in his writings, to observe the laws of perspective;— he tells you of objects, not as he knows them to be, but as they seemed to him.

—Alexander Kinglake, *Eothen*

For even as the Occident regards the Far East, so does the Far East regard the Occident,—only with this difference: that what each most esteems in itself is least likely to be esteemed by the other.

—Lafcadio Hearn, *Kokoro*

CONTENTS

ACKNOWLEDGMENTS

Parts of this work appeared, in different forms, in the International House of Japan Bulletin, Salmagundi, World Literature Today, and The Georgia Review. I am grateful for the hospitality of these periodicals.

In writing this memoir, I owe to many friends, acquaintances, strangers even, both Japanese and American, more than they or I realize. Let a few stand for all: Walter Abish, Peter Conrad, Shuichi Kato, Yoshiaki Koshikawa, Donald Keene, Robert J. Smith.

Several times, traveling to and from Asia, my wife, Sally Hassan, and I stopped with Marianne McDonald in San Diego. I thank her for her rare generosity, independence of mind, and cultural insights into Japan.

Finally, I wish to thank the following authors, translators, and publishers for permission to quote poetry extracts from Matsuo Basho, The Narrow Road to the Deep North and Other Travel Sketches, tr. Nobuyuki Yuasa (London: Penguin Classics, 1966); Makoto Ooka, Elegy and Benediction, trs. William I. Elliott and Kazuo Kamakura (Tokyo: Jitsugetsu-kan, 1991); Takashi Tsujii, A Stone Monument on a Fine Day, trs. Hisao Kanaseki and Timothy Harris (Tokyo: Libro Port Publishing, 1990); and Muso Soseki, Sun at Midnight, trs. W. S. Merwin and Soiku Shigematsu (San Francisco: North Point Press, 1989).

PREFACE

I stumbled, you might say blundered, into Japan. I could not claim, like Charlie Chaplin, that I went there because I once saw a Japanese actor walk magically across a stage. I went because someone invited me to lecture at the Kyoto Summer Seminars. That was 1974.

Summer in steamy Kyoto, a globe-trotting friend wondered? My wife, Sally, said, why not? I could never resist that query, its small defiance of fate. I could never decline an invitation to voyage. We went, a bit reluctantly, after tripping on maps around the house.

Like the child in Baudelaire's poem, "Le Voyage," I, too, was once "*amoureux de cartes et d'estampes.*" But that was in another country. I regard my birth in Egypt fortuitous, an accident, not a destiny. Call it an accident with resonances, memories. In any case, I never returned to Egypt. I came to America young and stayed. Japan? It seemed just another academic junket.

We returned to Japan ten times. Was Japan, then, more destiny, or at least destination, than Egypt? Indubitably. Still, as in everything crucial in this memoir, I triangulate: Japan, Egypt, America, my home.

I have learned in Japan a little about dispossession, homelessness. Hugo of St. Victor went further: "The tender soul has fixed his love on one spot in the world; the strong man has extended his love to all places; the perfect man has extinguished his." This would never persuade a true Egyptian—the Nile binds him like an umbilical cord—still less a true Japanese. Except perhaps a wanderer of eternity like Basho, who understood the contingency of all things in his marrow bones.

But for a plain American immigrant like myself, already once displaced, where does dispossession leave him? Between the Eagle and the Sun? Hardly. And just what lies between them? Less dying echoes of Egypt, I think, than aspirations of a life, prayers for clarity.

Clarity. Living in Japan in the fall of 1991, I started to write, though I knew Japanese language and life far less than others. I said to myself, this is not a book about them; it is a book about myself living among others. Living and seeing myself sometimes as another, because in Japan I will always remain a stranger on a far island. And because I have reached an age that makes my own life seem strange to me.

Writing in this humor, though, I found myself tracing a recognizable country, culture, people—not only "my Japan." The mood was sometimes anxious. I wrote "they," I wrote "them," I wrote distrusting generalizations. In any case, I did not address Japanologists, knowing that hell hath no fury greater than a specialist transgressed.

In the West, writing allows criticism. But how criticize Japan? In all my visits to that country, I encountered only courtesy, generosity, delicacy in welcome. Can criticism be the wages of hospitality? Recall, too, that relations between Japan and the United States are among the most crucial, geopolitically. (They were crucial from the start, when Commodore Matthew Perry initiated the first treaty Japan signed with the Occidental nations in 1854.) Why not shore up, rather than chip away, at these relations?

Even if we do want to criticize Japan, we soon realize that no criticism can really penetrate it. For that nation, despite—or perhaps because of—its acute sensitivities, lives in an invisible force field. If a gaijin (foreigner) criticizes Japan, he is gently asked, "Do you speak Japanese?" If he speaks Japanese fluently, he is requested, "Wakatte kudasai" (please understand) or, more emphatically, "Kangae naoshite" (please think it over). If he persists, he is discreetly reminded that, as a foreigner, he can never really apprehend the Japanese essence. In short, to understand is to approve, no further explanation necessary. To misunderstand is only to prove one's foreignness, no explanation possible. The force field is impenetrable; it deflects or repels all criticism.

But writing is more than praise or blame; it is also knowledge, empathy, delight. It is style. I have adopted here various styles, as mood and topic change, as Japan itself changes, compelling our perceptions of it to alter. Of course, no one really knows how deep or perdurable those changes will prove. And so I have repeated myself a little, just as Japan changes and remains the same. I have ventured to experiment a little with the book's form.

Mood, topic, style, form—let them shift and alter. I have no unifying concept, no paramount perception, of everything Japanese. But when I compare daily life in America and in Japan, the feel of things in each, I am struck by how much the idea of affluence rules the first, how much the idea of scarcity rules the latter. I mean scarcity, too, as it touches the notoriously ineffable Japanese concepts of *wabi* and *sabi*: the former with overtones of lament, discouragement, helplessness; freedom from worldly values; spiritual richness in poverty, in melancholy; an aesthetic and metaphysic of bittersweet sobriety— the latter with overtones of rust, dryness, paleness; avoidance of vulgar, mundane things; subtlety of humor as in haiku; loneliness, quietness, simplicity, profundity. . . .

Buddhist rarefications, you say? Well, look at an American plate in the days before our salad craze. The food rises in a heap, genially chaotic, caloric beyond human need. Two fat pork chops, mashed potatoes, buttered peas, all swimming in thick brown gravy. Generous, certainly, though some may say gross. Compare now with a Japanese plate. Where's the beef, where's the gravy? Instead, reticence and design: a few slices of fresh sashimi or an arc of sushi rolls, a gingko nut, sprig of pine or bamboo shoot, a tiny cone of ginger filleted into transparency. Yes, design, deftness, above all restraint. Or is it just lack, a kind of meanness in aesthetic dress?

America remains a culture of plenty, retaining the habits of waste, even if something now saps its will, its wealth. And Japan remains a culture of dearth, retaining the habits of want, though bullion now chokes its vaults. But how much can these symmetries finally explain? How much can they account for my own beguilements in the land of Yamato?

I discovered quickly that Japan invites enchantment, followed by slow disenchantment; the exotic always shows two faces. I began with the former, experienced the latter, and now find myself . . . exactly where? This book assays an answer, least assured in its abstractions, most in the people it portrays. The people—some close friends—abide when all the shadows of romance and exasperation have fled, the longer shadows of prophecy too.

I do not believe Japan holds the keys to this planet's future: I do not know if any nation does. Keys, the sages remind us, lie within. We jangle them in our pockets, carry them on journeys, risk something on the road, then return to unlock a banal casket, a familiar door. What key, what extraneous door? In Japan as in America, I have tried to shape my life, not the world. That same impulse drove me to revisit Japan, repeatedly, and to travel its byways with a head full of prejudices and amazement.

Travel begins in childhood dreams, and wise, old men die peregrine. But I sit now in a Swedish armchair to write, two soft, black cushions beneath me. I recall a line of Ogai Mori: "Neither fearing nor yearning for death, I walk down the descending slope of life."

But without the serenity of Ogai, I also think, when did my wanderings begin? Where did I swerve?

That swerve—is it not part of the road itself? The road took me to Japan. But I heard a cry behind me, Thoreau's "Simplify, simplify."

PART I
PREVIEWS

APPEARANCES

Nothing in Japan seems to be what it seems. Yet everything there is surface, appearance. Forms matter. You might say, the spirit killeth but the letter giveth life—only that wouldn't be exactly right.

The first thing I saw in Japan was people—silent swirls of people, vibrating in a field of sentient energy. Then I noticed faces, detaching themselves here and there from the unanimous crowd. For instance, at the old Tokyo airport, Haneda, a tiny cleaning woman in a white apron, age uncertain—say forty, or seventy-five—her body bent permanently at a right angle, skin tight on high cheekbones, black eyes intent as she sweeps trash with swift, gloved hands. It is an arresting, not a beautiful, sight.

Beautiful? Yes, the world lives in the eye; sight is primary, primary also in its prejudices. I'll say it plainly: I did not find the Japanese a handsome people. Not at first. My mind could not censor the visceral "fact." Everywhere I looked in the crowds, I saw short, stocky figures, thick ankles and wrists, bowed legs, heavy spectacles, lidded eyes. Perhaps I idealized limbs too much, being bowed in one leg myself. Perhaps I recalled too vividly those propaganda cartoons of Japanese soldiers, hiding in coconut trees or swarming Pacific beaches, pictures I had seen as a boy in Egypt. Or did I remember that character in a Tanizaki story who cries, "I have no confidence in my appearance, I'm small, I'm dark-skinned, and my teeth stick out in all directions"? Perhaps I was simply jet-dazed.

In any case, I did not feel, as travelers often do, sensuously, sensually, alive in Japan. Not in the beginning.

Then I started to note other visible facts. How deft the Japanese were in motion, how still in stillness. The gaijin, by contrast, lumbered like rhinos through undergrowth; even mentally, they seemed to bang and crash around. This Japanese economy of outer and inner motion struck me as a kind of spiritual elegance. I remarked also other somatic types: here a waist no thicker than some rednecks I have seen in America, there hands so delicate a butterfly might mistake them for a mate. Nearly everywhere, glossy, clean hair, luminously black, and smooth skin, unblemished in its various shades. Later, a decade or more later, I would realize how tall Japanese youth had become—fed at McDonald's, Shakey's, Colonel Sanders's, Mrs. Fields's?—how tall and lithe and slim. And how winsome, sometimes exquisite, women or men could be.

Still, still, my first impression lingered: the Japanese were inescapably an alien people, alien, say, as Chinese Americans had long ceased to be for me. Japanese bodies had a dynamic, a density, a shadowy space of their own. I could not project myself into that space. I accepted their distance, bowed without touching, held myself in reserve. I sensed, too, that their reserve contributed to my own. This reserve, theirs or mine, could become aloofness, even solitude.

The physical object strikes the eye, the imagination spins within. In erotic, political, or spiritual matters, fancy inspires its own facts. But in Japan, that first time, even my fancy seemed becalmed. I knew too little about the place, felt no compelling reason for being there—felt in fact a little absurd, as I would later, dressed formally in jacket and tie, standing in my socks on the tatami floor, conversing ceremoniously with strangers, wondering suddenly if my socks smelled, if they betrayed a darned hole, an incipient tear, and then thinking with subliminal irritation, "Doesn't all this squatting bend the shinbones?"

Tactless thoughts behind alien eyes. But the Japanese knew how to reciprocate: I probably appeared more alien to them than they appeared to me. And yet that woman at Haneda, her back a broken bow, might have stepped out, minus the gloves, of a farm tucked deep into my Egyptian past. Bearing ancestral memories, she also presaged all our hardening spines.

From the start, then, I saw Japan with puzzled, ambivalent eyes. The scene that greeted me as the airport car crawled through clotted traffic did not cheer or cleanse my sight. It was a flat scene of brown canals, barren embankments, high-rent tenements, rectilinear urban sprawls, bedizened with blocky kanji and looping hiragana signs. This was not the landscape of Utamaro, Hiroshige, Hokusai; it seemed, rather, Braque, Gris, Léger, painting "The Waste Land" through monochrome haze.

Appearances: they are blind to time. Contrary to all appearances, something in Japan impressed itself quietly, gradually, deeply, into some layer of my mind, like invisible writing, becoming slowly legible over the years. It was a message, below the surface of time, explaining my life somehow, explaining it to myself.

IWAO IWAMOTO

Iwao Iwamoto may have carried the first message.

He appeared one day, early autumn of 1966, in my office at Wesleyan University. He sat, a trim, shy figure in an armchair across from my desk, his tie slightly askew, and his small feet barely touched the carpet. He had just translated my first book, *Radical Innocence* (1961).

The Japanese wryly boast that they are themselves the richest natural resource of an indigent nation. Iwamoto is certainly natural and perhaps ingenuously nationalist: I have never heard him praise or blame Japan. He is a native treasure too. He teaches and travels much abroad, yet it would never occur to him, as it did desperately to me, to emigrate, and so to deny his *kuni* (ancestral place). After a month, say, in Milwaukee, he begins to hurt quietly, with unruffled resignation; he is missing Japanese food, sashimi and sushi, and, of course, white, glutinous rice, *gohan*.

Iwamoto shuns politics, never votes. A native of Kyushu, island of obdurate samurai who once fought both shogun and emperor, he remains unalterably pacific. Too young to join the Imperial Navy during the war, he survived the firebombings of Tokyo and Yokohama, where he attended school. Instead of a naval officer, he became a scholar of American literature. Later, as if by accident, he found himself one of the foremost Japanese scholars, teachers, translators, of that literature.

You can tell that he is a liberal Japanese: he never tightens the knot of his tie, and his graying hair, sometimes cut by one of his daughters, tumbles over his glasses, which he takes off to peer closely at a page. But with three daughters married now, Iwamoto has become a little patriarchic in his own wistful and sere way. He thinks less of cherry blossoms than of autumn leaves. The new Japan, which his lank, gangly students embody, puzzles him. But he does not admit to puzzlement; he only cocks his head, raises an eyebrow, and sometimes taps his heart, saying, "I'm very Japanese."

Something in Iwamoto was always autumnal, a falling cadence of life, a sense of time's hollowness, if not decay. That is a form Japanese decency takes, severity in nostalgia, refusal of color, *shibusa*. Sometimes I imagine seeing in Iwamoto's self-deprecating smile traces of ancient memories: fires, volcanoes, typhoons, earthquakes, bloody civil wars. I imagine in that acceptant smile the spirit of the great temple at Ise, rebuilt board by board every twenty years to honor the evanescence of existence. Nothing in the smile, anyway, evokes those horrid stereotypes, the toothy kamikaze, the sword-brandishing captain screaming, "Banzai!" At worst, if you speak nonsense, the smile goes quizzical and Iwamoto says, "Really?"

How different, this avoidance of argument, from the needs of my American, let alone voluble Egyptian, friends. From my own needs. Was that my reason for valuing Iwamoto all the more, a kind of distant, "Oriental cousin," if not brother, who evinces so little spiritual vulgarity, the quotidian bluster and assertiveness of my own milieu?

I have met Japanese, arrogant and vain behind their immaculate bows, offering their *meishi* (name cards) with impassive dislike. Yet with Iwamoto, as with many of his compatriots, courtesy is a kind of shyness, a delicacy before existence. It is a shyness or delicacy that can shade into the gruffness of Zen. At its very best, it becomes a cosmic courtesy. Was this part of the message Iwamoto brought me from Japan, on that New England autumnal day, back in 1966?

If so, the message still seems to me half garbled, barely legible.

BEWILDERMENTS: 1974

I flew from Seattle on a Boeing 747, with a whiff of dread. Perhaps it was excitement more than dread, the fine grit of adventure stirring, clouding my head. I wondered how Saint Francis Xavier had felt, in 1549, sailing on a Chinese pirate junk for Kagoshima, dreaming of Christian converts without number, all rising with him to heaven. But unlike the Apostle of the Indies, I knew heaven only at thirty thousand feet.

Arching over the Pacific in a great circle, I mused where mad Ahab had gone, and fathomless Moby Dick, their demesne drastically shrunk. "Nine hours and twenty-five minutes flying time, and we hope you enjoy your flight on Northwest Airlines." Had all mystery in the world fled? Or will the white whale live on forever in the hyperspace of our minds? I sat in my narrow plastic seat and meditated morosely on Ishmael's coffin.

I thought of America, too, receding eastward now, behind my back, though once I could imagine nothing west of that horizon of dreams. And I thought of Seattle, short hop to Alaska, with its wide, unlived spaces, its frontier seediness still visible in places, sensing one evening on a drizzly waterfront stroll a kind of derelict hopefulness, a rainy promise in the air. I had never been anywhere west—oh, except to California, of course—and I experienced Seattle as both the past, where the frontier had stopped, and the future, the still-uncrowded possibility of America, a coastland utopia beginning to gleam with glass and steel.

By the time I landed in Haneda, I fancied I had gone through a boundless mirror, the Pacific sky, and crossed into a world intangibly skewed. Japan a mirror image of America? Not quite; things were right-side there, except for traffic, trains, the way people passed you on the street. But it was always as if an Asian Cheshire Cat lurked around the corner, and a Nipponese March Hare whisked by while you were tying your shoe. I half expected to vanish in a shop window or a revolving door.

Odd serendipity: a book, a translation, a friend, and here I was in Japan.

It was mid July—though born in Cairo, I detest heat intemperately, as if it exhaled all the atavism of the race—the rainy, sweltering season in Japan. The first images that impressed themselves on me were commonplace; they simply sank in an overheated, expectant brain.

I recall, for instance, pasteboard policemen, with arms upraised and a thousand-yard stare, painted effigies at crowded intersections, reminding motorists that Authority is ubiquitous. I recall, on Ginza streets, arrays of gleaming, multicolored sunglasses, displayed on seven-foot-high revolving racks, something there for every louche or antic taste, no glasses ever pilfered. I recall models of dishes served in restaurants, their colors garish, waxen shrimp staring back at passers by, rubbery, decapitated eels ready to slither through the window. I recall in a bleak office courtyard, a rift of concrete really, all nature staged in a microcosm: a midget mountain, lake, islet, bonsai tree, meditating fisherman, everything perfectly proportionate. I recall a *pachinko* parlor, a sahara of nickel slot machines, the air impenetrable with cigarette smoke and the din of a million ratchets, levers, spinning wheels, and rolling steel balls, a haven for androids of every sex, class, and age—androids escaping humanity for an hour.

Such images were not allegorical; I did not know Japan enough to make them so. Two recollections, though, became more emblematic for me.

Once, on a visit to Osaka, Sally and I rambled through crowded, downtown streets. It was the empire of signs, shimmering in the midday, humid heat. Suddenly, Sally caught my arm, pointing to the top of a seven-story building across the roaring motorway. There, on the roof, side by side, stood a Shinto shrine, shaded by pines, and a large, squat air-conditioning machine. They were of equal size and equal status, seemingly locked together in daily, metaphysical converse. Sally laughed: "Another Virgin and Dynamo?" I answered: "But without Henry Adams's complaint."

The other memory is from a trip to the ancient capital, Nara, with its celebrated temples, Todaiji and Horyuji, its Daibutsu (Great Buddha), its Kasuga Shrine, its imperial red deer roaming freely in the gardens. Driving over from Kyoto with a Japanese friend, though, we traversed wastes of fumes and garbage, of asphalt, corrugated iron, shredded plastic. The trucks on the two-lane highway spewed hot, black clouds that rolled through our open windows. Courtesy struggled in our gasping lungs with the fumes. Finally, we put our handkerchiefs discreetly to our nostrils. Our guide pretended not to notice and I think never forgave us the gesture.

In the inner temple, various titular and protective deities surround the Buddha in his repose. Fierce, energetic figures guard the outer rectangle—the One All Seeing, the One All Hearing, Open Mouth Energy (Ah), Closed Mouth Energy (Em), the warriors Nikko and Gakko. Within, serene figures of contemplation encircle the Godhead, a void. I wondered, is this industrial belt surrounding Nara a grim parody of the protective rectangle framing the Buddhist altar? Or has the yen simply displaced Zen? Or is it, rather, that in its fanatic revanchism, Japan has committed ecological hara-kiri? Was this still the reverent land that designated ancient or giant, gnarled trees, *shimboku*, as sacred and draped great, straw ropes around their trunks?

My questions were not wholly rhetorical. Japanese science fiction abounded with fantasies of catastrophe: Japan turned into a polluted dump, begging the world to relocate one hundred million people—just where, after the vastations of the Imperial Army?—or Japan swallowed whole by the sea. Thus, Godzilla emerges from the mist of prehistory, a monster avatar, ready to battle enemies of the Rising Sun.

However unseductive Japanese urban landscapes seemed, other qualities, inner vistas, redeemed for me the blight: discipline; courage; loyalty; sacrifice; an adaptive genius; a meticulousness of the heart; an aesthetic tradition both simple and dazzling; asymmetry where it counts, at the center of things; delicacy in unexpected places, lighter than cherry blossoms in a breeze; a brown mournfulness beneath the skin; and yes, a spirit, a most troublesome spirit, of purity. Decidedly, Japan had something, something once crucial to society, that other nations now lacked.

It was something, when I came to recognize it, wholly sublunary, yet somehow preternatural, distilled of scarcity, sacrifice, ingenuity, distilled of time. It was something some Japanese claimed for themselves as the Japanese spirit, *Yamato damashii*, though when they claimed it, it could become demented. It was something at home in radical incongruities, say Technology and Shinto, and conversant with shadows. It was not intellectual, was sensuous rather, and evanescent. Roland Barthes glimpsed it in the "fissure même du symbolique." I saw it as well in dappled things, broken in their perfection, a lovely vase drab like rock, a quick brush stroke, part smear and part soul. Always, it was fashioned to the human measure, precisely, finally empty.

Japan, I have said, invites idealization and disgruntlement, and that summer I seemed to drift in and out of each. Tokyo had struck me with its immane vitality, its livid ugliness—the new architecture had not yet changed the cityscape—a colossal mart of services nearly infinite in their permutations. Sally and I had never experienced such consummate service or courtesy, even in the lowliest *soba* shop, hunkering beneath the rain-blotched concrete overpasses at Hibiya. Kyoto, not a breathtaking city in itself, filled our historical horizon almost too subtly. It was for us, that first time, a space of historical rumors, hidden rituals, beauties that refused to lay themselves bare.

The exception, perhaps, was the Gion Matsuri Festival, a raucous, motley affair, throbbing with primitive energies. Gorgeous, gilded, and grotesque floats paraded by, with their complements of uniformed retainers and sects. Some rolled on enormous wheels, pulled by as many as four hundred persons; others, palanquin-like, bounced or glided on the shoulders of wiry, gleaming men in loincloths. Begun in A.D. 876 to invoke divine protection against an epidemic, the festival still marches through time to the tunes of flutes and gongs and drums. In it, myth opens on history, and both open on the postmodern present. In Gion, as in so many village and city festivals, Japan took hold annually of its archaic self.

Gion was an exception. Perhaps I was callow, perhaps too intellectual, in my approach to Kyoto. I could savor celebrated sites: Daitokuji, the Temples of Silver and Gold Pavilions, the Katsura Detached Palace (by special permission), the Zen garden at Ryoanji. But I always felt there, more than I felt before the ancient monuments of Egypt, something at once hollow and concealed. I missed circular forms in traditional Japanese architecture, as I had missed them in Luxor or Thebes. But I reveled in Japanese diagonals, free contours, secret spaces. In a Japanese palace or temple yard, men surprised themselves and creation. In a Zen garden, like Ryoanji or Tenryuji, shrub, rock, and water could echo one another or mirror the sky, but the echo would hide a new note, the mirror flicker a new image. And at Nijo Castle, the wooden "nightingale floor" might sing to herald a Ninja assassin, but its aleatory song could inspire the music of John Cage or at least his great, silent laugh. Wood, paper, bamboo, light, even the thousand-year cedar, living materials, alive to climatic shifts, came close to animate grace. Everywhere: irregularity, change, the garden blending into architecture, temple and palace exemplifying a view of being, and all this centuries before the incomparable Muso Soseki perfected the temple gardens of Kyoto.

Sally, however, had her views of Japanese gardens. Yes, they offered a sensorium, appealing to sight, smell, touch, hearing— water over rocks, wind in the trees, deer scarers tinkling from post or transom. A sensorium of secret codes, almost Pynchonesque. But for her, the space lacked the romance of colors and smells in an English garden, and their shrubs often looked muddy green. It was all a little closed in, like an exquisitely designed vegetal tomb. Not, she quickly added, that Versailles enchanted her, or those Cartesian parks with their pebbled walks, bleached lawns, mannered statues smirking down from their pediments.

Perhaps we were still dragging our travel-worn, Western concepts—baroque, neoclassical, romantic—into a world with a different history, different people. True, the Japanese smiled as readily as Americans, but their smiles masked other moods, and their feelings, like their ages or accents, were often devilish to construe. Masked? We had promised ourselves to refuse that old myth of inscrutability, taking people as they come. They came courteously, from Shinto marriage to Buddhist burial, and all the Western technology in between failed to roil their manners.

From the instant we arrived on the *shinkansen* at Kyoto Station, a bit giddy from the light, lateral jiggle of bullet trains, we fell into the hands of Professors Aoki (Kyoto University) and Iwayama (Doshisha University), guardian angels who guided us through the intricacies of the Kyoto Summer Seminars. Privately, irreverently, we nicknamed them Nikko and Gakko. Gratefully, we accepted their help, though we found Japanese sociability at times intrusive. At such times, I would plead work and sneak to our diminutive, prefabricated room in the Palace-Side Hotel or take a sweaty evening walk in the Kyoto Gosho, deep gravel grinding beneath my sneakers at every step.

The work was real, the lecturing intensive. But my seminars often sputtered into silence after I introduced the topic. Japanese scholars specialized implacably, as did actors, physicians, car dealers. This specialization was an aspect of their meticulousness, even their purity; it did not make for brilliant converse. For the first time, I felt stymied in a seminar unless I could plant some senior professor to question me decorously. For the first time, I felt the "eros of ideas" (Whitehead) elude me. My students, younger colleagues really, had thought to please me with their ceremonious silence—except Professor Aoki, who liked to provoke me in a velvety voice.

Flattery is an ancient art in Japan, of course, geishas its consummate votaries. But common bar girls were hardly feckless in that same art. Late one evening, after a *shabu-shabu* dinner, Sally and I insisted that Iwamoto take us both to a Kyoto bar. We wandered through Higashiyama's entertainment district across the Kamo River, while Iwamoto studied various signs and nocturnal omens of the *mizushobai* (floating world or water trade) illegible to us. Suddenly he pointed, wagging his index finger. It was a bar, tiny and dark, up a flight of wooden steps into something like an air-conditioned treehouse. The girls, in neat summer dresses, were neither plain nor pretty, only genial, wholly at ease. They joked and teased, flattered affectionately, stroked Sally's hair, smiled sincerely. They admired, convincingly, everything we wore, said, or did. Then Iwamoto, who had interpreted for us with embarrassed whispers and grins, paid the exorbitant bill, and we left.

There, in the darkness of a small, nameless bar, the girls suddenly acted on me like a prism. Their lives may have been blithe or boring or simply venal, but they refracted clear hues of the Japanese social contract. Or perhaps they acted like those Japanese temple bells, treasured for their echo more than their knell. Whatever the metaphor, I sensed in Japan an extraordinary social quality—call it readiness in obligation, call it the art of service. Is it fanciful to compare that quality with America's old "willingness of the heart" (F. Scott Fitzgerald)?

A Japanese tobacconist who lacked a particular brand would call a cigar store five blocks away and accompany you, a stranger, to the competitor's door. A Seiko salesman, whether or not you bought from him a watch, would phone a central station for the precise time to set your old watch. An interviewer—later a friend, Keisuke Kawakubo—seeing you squirm under the TV kliegs, seeing you fidget, cough, mop your brow, would sit with you like a Buddha and smile till your own lymphatic system caught from him the cue. A host would make sure to take you for a pizza or hamburger after your official kaiseki dinner if you left most of it on the exquisite plates. A barber would switch the TV to an English-language channel the moment you entered his shop. In a small town, a taxicab company, too busy to answer a call, would send the owner himself, who refuses to take payment, crying in English, "Service! Service!" The examples are poignant, a touch comical, truly endless.

When I recall how bumptious and self-concerned human intercourse could be in other lands, I wonder if any society has achieved a denser, subtler, social contract. At a price, of course, at a price: conformity, exclusiveness, inhibited creativity, cruelty to others. "Social contract," some foreigners exclaim, "Those are workaholics in rabbit hutches."

Stereotypes, we know, conceal often a grain of insight. Yet even on my first visit to Japan, a decade before Japan bashing became an invitation to America bashing, I found in cultural clichés no measure of Japanese reality. How, then, did these global overachievers come to be what they are? Reaction to their isolation, dearth, defeat in the last war? History has never obeyed Newtonian mechanics. Baffled, I could only sense that the Japanese, as people, overshadowed all their monuments, Tokyo's energetic sprawl or Kyoto's supernal temples, overshadowed all the wonders of their technics. But I tried to resist my own bafflement: we always find in others the incongruities we seek. The bewilderments were all of my own making.

All this did not prevent Sally and me from breathing a sigh of cultural relief on the plane to Hawaii after our first three weeks in Japan. Honolulu glistened white in the Pacific, its air fresh, its flowers riotous, its proportions spacious. The pace was slower, the language or gesture mellifluous. Yes, Hawaiians were a handsome people.

Japan to Hawaii: from a technological nightmare to an arcadian dream? The question feeds only our nostalgia, our intellectual sloth. Besides, the year was 1974, and Japan had already begun to pervade Hawaii.

SUKI

My first visit to Japan seems now prehistoric. You want to see changes there, watch younger, no, middle-aged women. You can see in them what has and has not changed in Japan.

Take Suki, perhaps forty—but who can tell with those classic features, that taut skin over high cheekbones in a perfectly oval face, that thick, raven hair? I say Suki (for Sumiko), though most Western nicknames grate on older Japanese, because she likes her nickname, insists on it. A signal of internationalization? Not quite, not quite.

I first saw her sitting with her back to the hotel lobby, facing a blank, creamy wall. That was tact: she wanted her guests to face outwards. (In another age, the guest of honor sat back to corner, safe from an assassin's dagger or sword.) Suki waited, straight-backed, completely still—that's also Japanese. Besides, she knew that the hotel staff would lead us to her table. After all, her employer, the Chairman, owned the hotel as well as many other concerns, including a cultural foundation.

Suki had come to discuss with Sally and me an international conference. The conference never materialized; the Chairman gave it his silent, impeccably courteous avoidance. We did not blame him—who needed another academic conference? But Suki became a friend, a kind of friend. It was, you see, her first assignment on a new job, and we had all hit it off.

Why do I say "a kind of friend"? Because Suki's life did not belong to her; it belonged to the corporation. Weekdays and weekends, around the clock. She lived, I teased her, in the Cave of the Four Winds. As executive assistant to a creative, even whimsical, chairman, she coped with constant shifts in schedules, decisions, tactics, travel plans. I told her about Heraclitus's stream, and her laugh reminded me of scattered pearls. No matter, her tact and patience seemed inexhaustible, and she loved her job. Or did she?

The job pays handsomely, of course, for a Japanese woman. But that is the least of it. Fluent in several languages, Suki travels the world. She moves in the best circles, mingling business and culture, attentive to every human nuance, immaculately dressed. In designer grays and blacks and browns, she seems like an elegant wraith, always at the edge of sight, decisively at hand whenever needed. Paris, London, Moscow, New York, Cairo, Beijing, Los Angeles—she can deal with them all, without raising her voice.

But do not envy her. "When I enter a boardroom in London," she ruefully says, "all the men stand up." Suki's hand goes lightly to her heart. "But in Tokyo, they call and when I answer they curtly demand, 'A man in charge, please.'" Once, once only, to Sally, she said: "Where shall I ever meet my life companion? There's no time." Pause: "He doesn't have to be Japanese." She laughs. That's Suki: complete discretion, flashes of feeling.

Do not pity Suki either. If the deep exigencies of her work engulf her life, she has still made for herself a space without illusions. No tawdry mummeries of the self, no Murphy Browns here. Suki knows her mind, her heart. She knows where and when devotion matters. Ambiguously modern, ambivalently Japanese, she touches something more vital, more contradictory, in her society than, say, Masako Owada, future empress of the land.

PART II
THROUGH THE
LITERARY GLASS

TEXTS AND CONCEITS

There are many roads to knowing a country, and one high road runs through literature. I do not mean only travel books. I mean the kind of book that leaves you fretful, surly, or exalted, the kind that does not leave you at all. It remains often tacit, a bother somehow, even as you flip page after page. If you let it, it can take over your life.

There are many roads to knowing a country, and one of them involves comparisons, writerly juxtapositions, textual conceits. I have spent a good part of my life reading books. How better understand Japan now, I thought, than to contrast some of its literary works with American works I knew? Contrast? Call it stroking texts against each other's grain.

The first textual conceit conjoins Matsuo Basho's *The Narrow Road to the Deep North* with Walt Whitman's "Song of the Open Road."

Basho took several journeys, pilgrimages to places hallowed by their natural beauty or ancestral piety. He traveled, above all, to renew his own spirit, strewing verses as he tramped along, one foot in this world, the other, he said, in the next. Still, in the spirit of Zen, he drew his imagery from the taproots of the earth, the quivering instant, the mystic symbolism of *yugen*. He also averred: "No matter what we may be doing at a given moment, we must not forget that it has a bearing upon our everlasting self which is poetry"—note that he said "poetry," not "soul."

Indeed, poetry and Zen here happily blend. Variety is temporal and visible, unity eternal and concealed; both are real. In the same way, prose and poetry mingle in Basho's account, seeking ideal balance. Thus may we justly claim that The Narrow Road is a vision of eternity in perishable things, at once a hymn or orison to the cosmos and a murmur of Basho's mortality.

Scholars say he suffered much with diffidence. Others, given to so-called materialist nonexplanations, claim he journeyed to collect fees from his followers. In any case, travel was hard in his days, the roads perilous, his own ailments insistent. Yet he traveled, casting off his attachments, one by one, welcoming *sabi* and self-scrutiny. He traveled, nurturing in himself a "bit of madness," his poetry. This is the madness of deep perception, which permits him slyly to say:

> In a way
> It was fun
> Not to see Mount Fuji
> In foggy rain.

This is also the madness of a dispossessed man determined to become at last "a weather-exposed skeleton."

Basho's journeys—he often stopped, went home, only to start on the road again—are not equally compelling. His most poignant is the titular "The Narrow Road to the Deep North," which he commenced on 27 March 1689, at the age of forty-five, feeling older than his years, fearful of accumulating more frosty hairs on his head as he approached the cold mountains of Honshu. (In his lifetime, he may have walked more than three thousand miles.) The story starts: "Days and months are travellers of eternity. So are the years that pass by. Those who steer a boat across the sea, or drive a horse over the earth till they succumb to the weight of years, spend every minute of their lives travelling. There are a great number of ancients, too, who died on the road. I myself have been tempted for a long time by the cloud-moving wind—filled with a strong desire to wander." That sets the tone.

The desire to wander contains within it another desire: to die wandering and wondering, like the poets and sacred wayfarers of old. For Basho, Being never shows its beauty bare. It is mediated by every cherry blossom or frog in a pond. It is mediated as well by history, ancient sages, priests, heroes like the tragic warrior Lord Yoshitsune and his giant retainer, Benkei. It remains incarnate in the legacy of Japanese artists, past and present.

Indeed, one might carp that Basho's journeys are finally too retrospective and literary. But then, one might counter that even nature is artifice in Japan, that neither landscape nor history can escape there the coloring brush of mind. That is why Basho bursts into tears before the thousand-year-old monument at Taga Castle, its engraved letters barely visible through thick moss. This joyful moment, this tearful epiphany—frequent in Basho— is both a perception and an overcoming of alterity: the otherness of history mainly, which includes the "towering dead," the otherness of nature, too, with its crumbling mountains on the horizon, the otherness within oneself, the black crack in our selfhood. All this he achieves in the sordid midst of life:

> Bitten by fleas and lice,
> I slept in a bed,
> A horse urinating all the time
> Close to my pillow.

The journey is endless, and from mediation, the slippage of Being, there can be no surcease. The last poem Basho writes on his voyage north is an invitation to a new voyage.

Walt Whitman wrote *Leaves of Grass* some two centuries after Basho, but he serves better than, say, Anne Bradstreet as the haiku master's counterpart. Let us hear the "Song of the Open Road" through echoes of Basho's words. Whitman commences:

> Afoot and light-hearted, I take to the open road,
> Healthy, free, the world before me,
> The long brown path before me, leading wherever I choose.

This stanza (of thirty-five syllables) could swallow two haiku whole and still have one syllable to spare. Its singer is no "weather-exposed skeleton" or "travel-worn satchel" but a brash Camden seer who declaims:

> I myself am good fortune. . . .
> I am larger, better than I thought;
> I did not know I held so much goodness.

There is a whole history, geography, culture in these words, a whole way of being that makes *wabi* or *sabi*—the melancholy of rust, the solitude of dry autumn leaves—altogether superfluous.

Whitman, I said, declaims. He does more; he assumes continually a "You," a democratic reader. In fact, he more than assumes: he hails, accosts, harangues, impetrates, increpates, exprobates, and generally importunes that reader. These sublime apostrophes create an intimacy and, as in all intimacies, an irritation that Basho avoids. The intimacy, though, remains somehow abstract. Perhaps this is the abstraction of democratic ideals mistaken for actual feelings. Perhaps it is the abstraction of thought itself.

Thought? Does not Basho think? He thinks best as nature thinks, in images, in objects, in the silences of sensuous apprehension. By comparison, Whitman's poetry seems chaste in natural imagery. Its large statements roll with emotions, human energies of another kind. Thus, chaste as it may be in one respect, it is far sexier than Basho's:

> These yearnings, why are they? These thoughts in the
> darkness, why are they?
> Why are there men and women that while they are nigh
> me, the sun-light expands my blood?
> Why, when they leave me, do my pennants of joy sink flat
> and lank?

For Basho, such admissions of "the shuddering longing ache of contact" would be inconceivable. Nor, in a thousand Buddhist incarnations, could Basho end a poem as Whitman does:

> Mon enfant! I give you my hand!
> I give you my love, more precious than money.

It is not only a matter of didactic endings; their ways diverge as well. Both poets attempt a journey of the soul, passing through death, beyond death. But Basho rambles and Whitman surges. The latter continually adjures his readers, "forever alive, forever forward," promising them eternal struggle and vision supernal in the same breath. The enormous dynamism of Whitman's poem, despite its flaccid lines and *longeurs*, carries us through. His famous catalogs emulate the method of the avalanche. By contrast, Basho flits like a dragonfly or ripples like a stone tossed on a pond without shores.

The two poets, though, have their odd sympathies. They like to write under an open sky. They believe in dispossession: "Gently," Whitman says, "but with undeniable will, divesting myself of the holds that would hold me." They believe in the power of things unseen, and take the cosmos on its own terms:

> I do not want the constellations any nearer;
> I know they are very well where they are.

(I can imagine Basho wincing on hearing this, then nodding with a puckered smile.)

But these clandestine affinities should not lull our sense of variance. Basho, feeling wizened and decrepit, may take a close disciple on the road, may even indulge occasionally in a "banquet" of poetry. Whitman, boasting health, is more generic, promiscuous: "*Allons!* whoever you are, come travel with me!" Basho, in life as in literature, refines, selects, distills; Whitman roughens, clutters, embraces it all in. The Japanese poet venerates the past in his bones; the American shakes it off like a threadbare coat. His great companions are not bards or heroes of old but the emergent democratic multitudes in whom the "efflux of the Soul is happiness." In brief, Basho excludes, Whitman includes. It seems an old story: America, a continent with only a prehistory, Japan, an island with more history than it needs; the one acquiring more history than it can manage, the other forgetting selectively its past.

That both texts are poetic journeys is small serendipity. In the Japanese tradition, journeys rarely become discovery or exploration; they are, rather, exercises in poetic or spiritual recall. As Yasunari Kawabata put it, "It is part of the discipline of the different arts of Japan, as well as a guidepost to the spirit, for a man to make his way in the footsteps of his predecessors, journeying a hundred times to the famous places and old sites, but not to waste time traipsing over unknown mountains and rivers." This ethos contrasts markedly with the American mythos of the Territory Ahead.

But these are stark conclusions. I had meant to suggest something of the disparate cultural traditions of Japan and America, letting literature speak through cadences of its own, without too much ideological noise from "bat-eyed and materialistic priests" (Whitman). I chose Basho and Whitman because, though they do not subsume their respective cultures, they do convey something crucially vital in each.

In the same spirit of playful incongruence, I take up the next two exemplary essays, Junichiro Tanizaki's "In Praise of Shadows" and Norman Mailer's "The White Negro," separated not by two centuries but two decades. Both address the contemporary world; each defines a stance that we recognize intuitively—and, yes, a little stereotypically—as "Japanese," as "American."

Tanizaki's essay celebrates above all the deep penumbra of the Orient. The American architect Louis Kahn once remarked, "The sun never knew how wonderful it was until it fell on the wall of a building." By contrast, Tanizaki gives us a muted rhapsody of Japanese shades and shadows: in shoji (paper screens), wood, lacquer, food, silence, human skin. He discerns tenderly the "countless layers of darkness," the "sheen of grime," "the pensive lustre," the "patina of age," the "cloudy translucence" of things all around him—including wooden Japanese toilets.

I am at a loss. Shall I cite the delightful passages on Japanese toilets, kitchens, paper, or skin? The last entails a curious reflection:

But what produces such differences in taste? In my opinion it is this: we Orientals tend to seek our satisfactions in whatever surroundings we happen to find ourselves, to content ourselves with things as they are; and so darkness causes us no discontent, we resign ourselves to it as inevitable. . . . But the progressive Westerner is determined always to better his lot. From candle to oil lamp, oil lamp to gaslight, gaslight to electric light—his quest for a brighter light never ceases, he spares no pains to eradicate even the minutest shadow.

But beyond such differences in temperament, I should like to consider the importance of the difference in the color of our skin.

Tanizaki then proceeds to comment on "the darkness that lay below the skin," the "gray shadow" and black hair of the Japanese, concluding: "Because no one likes to show himself to bad advantage, it is natural that we should have chosen cloudy colors for our food and clothing and houses, and sunk ourselves back into the shadows."

A fanciful conclusion perhaps, but one that is neither simple nor self-serving. For Tanizaki's essay is nothing if not subtly dialogical, ironic about itself, anti-Manichaean. Shadow, for one thing, requires both darkness and light, an interplay of both. For another, brightness outside may conceal darkness within the heart, as in the benighted West, Tanizaki hints. Then again, inside their world of shadows, far in its depths, the Japanese have "placed woman, marking her the whitest of beings." In any case, Tanizaki admits, the shadows belong to the past. Japan now consumes more electricity than any nation except America; its cities, neon-lit to the sky, are by far the brightest, the gaudiest. That, in fact, is why he fears the westernization of Japan. Yet even in his fear, Tanizaki appears full of slyness, self-deprecation, and nuance, as he engages the overbearing present:

> I am aware of and most grateful for the benefits of the age. No matter what complaints we may have, Japan has chosen to follow the West, and there is nothing for her to do but move bravely ahead and leave us old ones behind. But we must be resigned to the fact that as long as our skin is the color it is, the loss we have suffered cannot be remedied. . . . [But] I would call back at least for literature this world of shadows we are losing. In the mansion called literature I would have the eaves deep and the walls dark, I would push back into the shadows the things that come forward too clearly, I would strip away the useless decoration.

In that mansion belongs "In Praise of Shadows." The essay is indeed a Japanese kind of literature, personal without being self-vaunting, ruminative, vagrant in structure, full of little memories, confessions, anecdotes, "following the brushstroke," as the Japanese say. It is also autumnal in mood, espousing, as its translator notes, "an essentially pessimistic aesthetic, the aesthetic not of a celebrant but of a mourner," one who values the past over the future, meditation over action, in-direction at any cost—a man, though, quizzical about his own unworldly ways, and ready to see the brightness every shadow casts.

The mere mention of Mailer's menacing essay, "The White Negro," let alone its yoking with Tanizaki's, jangles the nerves. Yet Mailer, playing on black and white, also praises shadows as he engages the present. These, however, are the shadows of the American psyche, which gathered around the Beats in the fifties and which Mailer embodied in the prophetic figure of the hipster, raw existentialist of the American night. But prophetic of what? Certainly of the sixties, all their mock apocalypses and raucous liberations, prophetic too of this vast, violent, overripe dream we call America, perhaps prophetic of our whole world.

Mailer, we may recall, begins his fulgurant jeremiad by denouncing contemporary life, all the manifestations of a once Faustian, now death-driven, civilization, feeding on a hideous wound in man himself:

> It is on this bleak scene that a phenomenon has appeared: the American existentialist—the hipster, the man who knows that if our collective condition is to live with instant death by atomic war, relatively quick death by the State as l'univers concentrationnaire, or with a slow death by conformity with every creative and rebellious instinct stifled (at what damage to the mind and the heart and the liver and the nerves no research foundation for cancer will discover in a hurry), if the fate of twentieth-century man is to live with death from adolescence to premature senescence, why then the only life-giving answer is to accept the terms of death, to live with death as immediate danger, to divorce oneself from society, to exist without roots, to set out on that uncharted journey into the rebellious imperatives of the self.

Henceforth, the world divides into Hip and Square; darkness and light rarely meet in a chiaroscuro of the spirit. Can we be surprised? In Mailer's antic Manichaeanism, God and the devil play out their cosmic drama, part Grand Guignol and part farce, till the end of time.

I do not mean to belittle Mailer's talent. His essay, taut with mean insights, can cut and crack like a lash—note the rippling sentence quoted above. His hipster wounds our social, indeed our personal, self-esteem as he prowls the underground of culture—jazz, sex, drugs, crime, madness—for victories we may be too enervated to realize. Having "absorbed the existentialist synapses of the Negro" and thus become "a white black," the hipster confronts us with all we have concealed from ourselves and one another. That he is Mailer's alter ego in dark shades should not obscure the garish truths of his critique.

Whether Mailer's psychopath has served or might yet serve as "the perverted and dangerous front-runner of a new kind of personality," a shinjinrui, as the Japanese might say, remains moot. His individual rage, we might concede, mirrors something berserk in the age and is surely less ravaging than the collective frenzy of the State. In taking this view, Mailer proves himself an American romantic, a hip Rousseauist, anxious to return us to our radical element, the spontaneous criminal in us all—the brave, old, sinning self against the world.

There is nothing strenuous in discerning the new-world qualities of Mailer's essay or in remarking his personal signature, the calligraphy of a brilliant megalomania, on the text. The rhetoric of the inner self—of prophetic rebellion, visionary politics, utopian violence, and redemptive eroticism—would dumbfound Tanizaki into courtly silence. (Only in Yukio Mishima's work can we sometimes hear similar rhetorical overtones.)

And yet, are Tanizaki's and Mailer's essays really antipodal? Are they not both studies in the penumbra of mind, the shadow side of the modern world, the warps—I almost said kinks—of life? And do they not both follow the movement of an intuition, the "stroke of the brush" again, rather than develop a sustained argument? In doing so, Tanizaki murmurs and Mailer raves—I slightly exaggerate—to save us from ourselves. Far more crucially, Tanizaki, despite his courtly ironies, finally embraces his cultural tradition; his critical distance from it is slight. Mailer, by contrast, questions radically the assumptions of his Western moment, presuppositions that Tanizaki would find invisible in his own milieu.

So far, I have tried to intimate, through meshed parallels and contrasts, something of the nature, the quiddity, of Japanese and of American literature. In that mesh, parallels stand out less than contrasts, as befits the historical case. I come now to my third and final conceit: Kobo Abe's *The Box Man* and Donald Barthelme's *The Dead Father*. Other pairings of novels, cognate in theme, would have been as plausible: say Carson McCullers's *The Ballad of the Sad Café* and Yasushi Inoue's *The Hunting Gun*, or John Updike's *Rabbit Run* and Kenzaburo Oe's *A Personal Matter*. The fictions of Abe and Barthelme, however, elicit best those convergences of style and attitude notable in international postmodernism.

The Box Man is an aggressively—some would say egregiously—postmodern text. All the appurtenances of the "metafictional muse" are here: photos, lists, diagrams, newspaper captions, typographic variations, interstitial poems, diary entries, dream sequences, self-reflexive comments, shifting temporal schemes, unreliable narrators (one speaker is presumably a dead doctor) authorial intrusions of every kind—not to mention the obligatory irony, parody, pastiche, and deadpan humor. Meticulous, maniacally precise, the style weaves meaning and absurdity into a seamless verbal texture, with some shades of Barth, Beckett, Kafka, and perhaps Barthelme. Still, *The Box Man* remains a masterpiece of its kind.

This is largely, I think, because the book raises the hackneyed dialectic of contemporary alienation to the condition of an original, an agonizing mystery. Self and society, same and other, dissolve into an ever-changing gaze, the look, the looker, and the looked upon becoming now one, now many, as each box man within his slitted box—including the reader—looks upon the world both to recover and lose his identity. Thus voyeurism—erotic, artistic, social, metaphysical—becomes the glaring metaphor of this Eye Novel/I Novel (weird *shi-shosetsu* indeed) about a photographer turned into the denizen of a cardboard box.

The metaphor shifts. To inhabit a box in stark dispossession is to lose one's social identity, become an invisible man. This is tacit resistance, the freedom of anonymity. But to see without being seen is also to put one's identity in jeopardy. That is why every box man, every seer, must also be seen—seen, say, by the young nude nurse in the novel, or by a double, or by the author who sees his characters, or by the reader who sees the author, or, finally, by language itself, myriad-eyed, which "sees" everyone through countless words.

Certainly, the box man is a resister, a reject; rejecting society, he also lives with its refuse. The box may be his Beckettian cranium or cardboard womb. Still, he is the perfect nonconsumer; recycling the dreck of society, he becomes himself part of its dreck. No vagrant or beggar, he is, as Abe tells us, the eternal victim in us all. But this victim is also full of foreboding and threat. Like his author, the narrator is master of sinister manipulations, which include fictive murder.

Indeed, death in the novel provides the final critique of postmodern society, its media and simulacra. The critique follows an interesting logic. Box men, it seems, favor portable radios—Sonys, no doubt—within their boxes. These pariahs, paradoxically, are addicts of world news. For as the narrator says, if you can't hear the noise of the world—or transfix its madness with your gaze—the world itself may dissolve. One day, however, the speaker's addiction to news suddenly ceases when he sees a man crumple dead before his box. The man is no one in particular, his death is "absolutely no news." But the banal event shocks the narrator into a realization of the root irrelevance of all news. The postmodern world thus seems to be held in place by news that ignores the only news that finally matters: the tidings of one's own death.

Toward the end, Abe seeks half-heartedly to resolve the exigencies of reality into some hope of love, hope of "almost love." But love does not endure; the box man returns to his box; the novelist—the prime box man himself—returns to the labyrinth of language. In ambiguous conclusion, the box man says to his mistress: "Apparently you're incapable of understanding. This is a tale, of course. This story is in the act of taking place. . . . The important thing is not the end. The thing to consider is the reality of your feeling the fiery wind on your skin. The denouement is not the problem. Now the fiery wind itself is important. . . . This is a rare time when a man can see with his eyes the soul as substance." This may be a man speaking cryptically to his mistress, or an author to his reader; it is, in any case, all that Abe can muster as postmodern affirmation. The "fiery wind" brings no perceptible change.

What can we recognize in all this as Japanese? Surely not the "human condition," or the international protocols of postmodernism. Barthelme, who answers nothing, may help us to answer this query. His The Dead Father is, of course, a dreckful enigma, a trash-filled riddle, an exhaustive mystery. It is also a fragment de longue haleine, a literary pastiche, a parodic quest epic, a collage of knowledge, and an allegory of our times, representing nothing. The Dead Father, neither dead nor really a father, may stand for God, History, Reason, Patriarchy, Modernism, Language, Authorship, all or none or some of the above. What is certain—I should say, almost certain—is that Barthelme's narrative moves, informs, reveals, perplexes, delights, and that we call it literature. For instance, this opening passage:

> The Dead Father's head. The main thing is, his eyes are open. Staring up into the sky. The eyes a two-valued blue, the blues of the Gitanes cigarette pack. The head never moves. Decades of staring. The brow is noble, good Christ, what else? Broad and noble. And serene, of course, he's dead, what else if not serene? From the tip of his finely shaped, delicately nostriled nose to the ground, fall of five and one half meters, figure obtained by triangulation. The hair is gray but a young gray. Full, almost to the shoulder, it is possible to admire the hair for a long time, many do, on a Sunday or other holiday or in those sandwich hours neatly placed between fattish slices of work. Jawline compares favorably to a rock formation. Imposing, rugged, all that. The great jaw contains thirty-two teeth, twenty-eight of the whiteness of standard bathroom fixtures and four stained, the latter a consequence of addiction to tobacco, according to legend, this beige quartet to be found in the center of the lower jaw. He is not perfect, thank God for that.

Now compare with an opening passage from The Box Man:

Instructions for Making a Box

MATERIALS:
1 empty box of corrugated cardboard
Vinyl sheet (semitransparent)—twenty inches square

Rubber tape (water-resistant)—about eight yards

Wire—about two yards

Small pointed knife (a tool)

(*To have on hand, if necessary: Three pieces of worn canvas and one pair of work boots in addition to regular work clothes for streetwear.*)

Any empty box a yard long by a yard wide and about four feet deep will do. However, in practice, one of the standard forms commonly called a "quarto" is desirable. Standard items are easy to find, and most commercial articles that use standard-sized boxes are generally of irregular shape—various types of foodstuffs precisely adaptable to the container—so that the construction is sturdier than others. The most important reason to use the standardized form is that it is hard to distinguish one box from another. As far as I know, most box men utilize this quarto box. For if the box has any striking features to it, its special anonymity will suffer.

Both novels flaunt their demented sense of detail. But there are differences—"thank God for that"—there are differences. As character, the Box Man remains plausible, in his abstract and finicky fashion realistic; his cold, first-person intimacy with the reader preserves distance. The Dead Father is by comparison Bunyanesque, a tall tale come to monstrous life, a swashbuckling hyperbole oozing pathos at every pore, a caricature as vital as Godzilla but infinitely more crafty and lewd. Paradoxically, this omniscient narrator attains greater familiarity with the reader, in a winking, rib-poking ambience of casual mayhem and jocose cruelty. Hence the effect of the Japanese novel, as a whole, is one of scrupulous necessity, lucid constriction; that of the American, emotional extravagance, festive absurdity. Acutely intelligent both, the first understands malice and defeat; the latter understands them as well, with a touch of adolescent bravado, turning death into carnival. Though ambiguities rule both fictions, both project kindred feelings about the facticity of contemporary life, East or West, and about metaphysical abandon. But these random affinities disguise differences that remain emblematic.

I realize that I have barely stroked the surface of two complex—I almost said capricious—works, at once velvety and grainy in texture, elusive in their depths. But I hope the point about difference stands: in an age of cybernetic crossbreeding, American and Japanese fiction seem to remain stubbornly distinct, as the cultures themselves remain distinct. Such distinctness, though, never rules out subtle complicities behind our backs.

Hints of complicity, perhaps also of hype—signposts in hybrid times—emerged in a recent dialogue between Jay McInerney and Haruki Murakami, sponsored by PEN in New York. Murakami, though a multi–*mirion sera* (million seller) in Japan, has lived long in the Occident, and his fiction crackles with references to American high and pop culture. He recollects:

> In the 1960s, when I was a teen-ager in Kobe, I found that I didn't like Japanese novelists much, so I made up my mind not to read them. . . .
>
> American culture was so vibrant back then, and I was very influenced by its music, television shows, cars, clothes, everything. That doesn't mean that the Japanese worshipped America, it means that we just loved *that* culture. It was so shiny and bright that sometimes it seemed like a fantasy world.

McInerney replies by alluding to a "reservoir of international pop culture" on which writers in Europe, America, and Asia now draw. "I sense," he says, "a poignant urge to roll over Buson and Basho, two of Japan's greatest poets, and to crash through the cultural gap that separates Japan to some extent from the rest of the world." Murakami, however, qualifies, demurs: "It's not as though I am after a sense of non-nationality. If that were really what I was after, I think maybe I would have set my novels in America. . . . But, you see, what I wanted was first to depict Japanese society through that aspect of it that could just as well take place in New York or San Francisco. You might call it the Japanese nature that remains only after you have thrown out, one after another, all those parts that are altogether too 'Japanese.' " Murakami may have it right, the right kind of difference, without the blather of Japanese "uniqueness."

But how understand Murakami in the scheme of our textual conceits? Put another way, how understand his immense success in Japan, a phenomenon they call Murakami madness? Has Japan really changed drastically since the war, or is the change merely a mirage of images, a trance of self-induced hype?

The questions concern the nature of postindustrial societies and concern America as well as Japan. Thus, for instance, the French sociologist Jean Baudrillard writes in his antic book, *America:* "America has no identity problem. In the future, power will belong to those peoples with no origins and no authenticity who know how to exploit that situation to the full. Look at Japan, which to a certain extent has pulled off this trick better than the U.S. itself, managing, in what seems to us an unintelligible paradox, to transform the power of territoriality and feudalism into that of deterritoriality and weightlessness. Japan is already a satellite of the planet Earth. Whether we like it or not, the future has shifted towards artificial satellites."

Pies or satellites in the sky aside, a different kind of literary work has now found its audience in Japan. The work, as in

Murakami's case, often makes the top of the best-seller list. It can be fiction at the edge of pop, or it can be serious fiction, postmodern fiction, that hostile critics label "pop." Sometimes the work cultivates tedium, inchoateness, transcendent banality; at other times, it surrenders to a frenzy of slapstick and pastiche. Such techniques may serve an emergent social vision with sullen or clownish art.

In fact, following the earlier Japanese modernists like Kawabata and Tanizaki, later than Mishima and Yasushi Inoue, younger still than Abe or Kenzaburo Oe, a generation of ambiguously gifted urban writers now struggles to render the febrile realities of Japan. Murakami heads that generation, as he does the hip anthology that his own translator, Alfred Birnbaum, edited and appropriately called *Monkey Brain Sushi* (1991).

In a brief, perceptive preface, Birnbaum limns some features of the new writers. Born and raised in Americanized postwar Japan, they are at ease with hamburgers and jeans, with miso soup and tatami mats. Their language itself has been anglicized: they prefer fuikkushon (fiction) to jun bungaku (pure literature). Steeped in Hollywood movies, rock music, television series, comic books, computer games, they seem savvy in the byways of the information (or disinformation) age. Thus, as Birnbaum says, "the background noise running through their writing attests to the incredible speed and volume at which anything 'new' and 'different' is now sought out, reprocessed, and marketed for mass dissemination, flattening entire cultures into appealing designs in the Japanese consumer mind."

This, then, is the cool matrix of Murakami's books, cool and flat like his prose. Does it make for a stunted literature? The answer is equivocal. Some of his earlier works seem no less numb than the characters they portray. The author's imagination perceives everything as in a glass smokily: soot and rain hang in the air. But with *A Wild Sheep Chase* (1982, tr. 1989), which earned the Noma Literary Award for New Writers, and with *Hard-Boiled Wonderland and the End of the World* (1985, tr. 1991), winner of the prestigious Tanizaki Prize, Murakami became both a best-seller and a grudging critical success. *Norwegian Wood* (1987, tr. 1990) confirmed him in both regards.

Norwegian Wood also speaks best to our point, a textual conceit in itself, commingling East and West, from its Beatle song title to its trailing "Japanese" inconclusion, refusing the symmetry of beginnings and ends. The novel is the first person story of Watanabe's initiation, moral education, like Fitzgerald's *Great Gatsby* or Salinger's *Catcher in the Rye*, both crucial, recurrent motifs in the book. The characters, mostly Tokyo students during the late sixties, early seventies, try to make sense of their loves and their lives, much as students would in Paris or New York. The quiet narrator, shy, solitary, self-absorbed—a type that has become the author's signature—conveys the sense of spiritual drift in that world.

This spiritual drift is both global and local. It shares in the alienation of youth everywhere, but it also has a distinct, duskier hue. For death and madness pervade the novel—four young people commit suicide, two suffer bouts of insanity. Indeed, suicide and madness become elusive gestures, claiming the brightest and the best, forms of intransigence, of purity even, that the Japanese traditionally find unbearably beautiful. What, after all, holds more glamour than the Void, Mu, the Abyss of which all things are made?

Murakami acknowledges the music of mortality, intrinsic to life itself yet sudden like a heart stab. There is something musical as well about the crumpled lives of the characters who join in a song of loss and solitude, inspired by "Norwegian Wood." As a wise character called Reiko, a former mental patient, says, the

Beatles "know a thing or two about life's sorrow and elegance." In such sorrows, though, begin responsibilities, even if no truth, strength, or grace can ever soothe the pain of final loss. "You should take responsibility for your decisions," repeats Reiko to Watanabe, whose beautiful, deranged love, Naoko, has committed suicide. "Otherwise nothing is worth anything." Watanabe already knows. Unlike his best friend, Kizuki, Naoko's former boyfriend, he opts for that compromise we call life: "Hey, Kizuki," he cries toward the end, "unlike you I've decided to live. And not just live, I've decided to make a go of it. . . . I'm no teenager. I've got responsibilities."

In sorrows, then, rather than in dreams, as Yeats thought, begin responsibilities for Murakami, at least in *Norwegian Wood*. The ideal calls for human relatedness rather than self-creation (Fitzgerald's Jay Gatsby) or the simple truth (Salinger's Holden Caulfield, or his livelier, tougher avatar, Huck Finn). Why then impute nihilism to Murakami, even if some of his characters seem drugged, reaching for a beer or performing sex as if in a trance?

Despite its adaptive genius, Japan may have experienced modernization more acutely than any other nation—from a medieval to a postindustrial society in barely one hundred years. The gash between generations can be hurtful, even if old courtesies serve as salve. For at least half a century, Japanese youth has seemed, like Matthew Arnold's Victorian speaker in "Dover Beach," between two worlds, "one dead, the other powerless to be born." No wonder that some Murakami characters give themselves lazily to nihilism, or choose the dark. No wonder they imagine falling into a deep well, "awfully deep . . . a black stew of all the varieties of darkness in the world."

This hidden and ubiquitous well may recall briefly the cliff before which the Catcher stands guard in the rye to save children from tumbling down to their deaths. But the well is within, and no one in *Norwegian Wood* seems able to save others from their doom. Thus, Murakami avoids the potential sentimentality of Salinger's celebrated novel, only to court a more stoical sentimentality of his own. Or is Murakami's stoicism the form truth must take in his world? Thus, Midori, another university student: "Say what you will, but when your only Father and Mother die on you or go off somewhere, aren't you supposed to feel something? With me, it's no good. I don't feel anything, not sad, not lonely, not bitter—such feelings hardly even cross my mind."

Perhaps the mood of these young characters, perhaps the mood of fictional remembrance itself, is what Murakami means by the "Japanese nature" that remains after we dispense with what is "altogether too 'Japanese.' " Fashion, class, ennui, personal status, the posturing of student radicals, the gossip of prurient neighbors, the mournful frolics of sex, the larger intricacies of love and remorse—all these are readily recognizable to an American reader, however distant from the scene. But the texture of melancholy, the readiness to sacrifice and will to responsibility—these define for Murakami the particular qualities of Japanese grace.

Where, then, do we find ourselves after all these textual conceits? Literature yields no worthy concepts like Ruth Benedict's Shame and Guilt cultures to explain Japan and America—the young in both countries resist her schemas now—or even casual notions of Dearth and Waste cultures, such as I insinuate in this work. Still, literature seems to breathe the qualities of these cultures and to speak to us beyond contrastive rubrics: say Japanese restraint and American gusto; or *shibui* (rooted in astringency, flowering into sober elegance) versus flash; or again, *mono no aware*

(an attitude of self-awareness in transience, sensitive resignation to mutability, perhaps even celebration of it) against Yankee willfulness.

Emerson was close to the mark: "An imaginative book," he said in his essay on "The Poet," "renders us more service, at first, by stimulating us through its tropes, than afterward, when we arrive at the precise sense of the author." But my words have mediated the tropes. Basho, with Emerson's blessings, offers the unmediated way: "Go to the pine if you want to learn about the pine, or to the bamboo if you want to learn about the bamboo. And in doing so, you must leave your subjective preoccupation with yourself." That is the poet's way, and it may be on some days the traveler's.

KOJIN KARATANI

He is no poet, rather an ideologue. He may be the intellectual's intellectual in Japan.

I see him squinting slightly, eyes close together, through dense cigarette smoke. Or perhaps through a haze of Marxist abstractions. I see him also listing slightly as he walks, as if mildly inebriated or suffering from a permanent jet lag.

He met me in the lobby of the Okura Hotel, and we walked into the Orchid Bar. Sumo in progress on a mammoth television in the corner. Karatani shifted his chair to turn his back on the screen. He ordered a Kirin, lit a cigarette, and began talking intensely about "exteriority."

Later, I walked him to the front entrance. A procession of bellhops, business executives, diplomats glided through the noiseless glass-and-brass doors. As we queued up for a taxi, I remarked facetiously on the parade of power. "Shitheads," Karatani hissed under his breath. A moment later, he lurched sullenly into his cab.

I reflected on how much of extremist politics seems personal, an old bitterness in the heart that the wicked world obliges. Thus Georg Lukács admits, in *History and Class Consciousness*, the "hatred and contempt I had felt for life under capitalism ever since my childhood." First childhood hatreds, then magisterial critiques of society?

But Karatani is also captive of a tradition, an elaborate genre: leftist politics in Japan. It is a tradition most Japanese consider now irrelevant. Still, it maintains itself as a consumer fad, a kind of designer socialism or angry chic. For instance: Karatani, in black turtleneck sweater, scowling his way through the glossy pages of *Switch* magazine.

Unfair, unfair to Karatani, unfair to Oe—but the latter is another story. Karatani is intelligent, serious, vain, naive. He reads everything, and it all comes out the same, bent inexorably by his needs. In English, his prose reads like a bad translation from the French. But, then, he reads French in English or Japanese.

The point is, what can the Left really do now in Japan? Posture, of course, like the Right. Or dump on Mishima. Or dream back the sixties. But there is much to be done. Only the ideologues, like old socialist politicians and unionized teachers, seem trapped in the amber of history.

Oe, a friend of Karatani—how friendly can two difficult men really be?—is another story. I do not refer simply to the Nobel Prize, awarded him in 1994, which thrust him into the intolerable glare of publicity precisely because his compatriots had almost ceased to read or remember him. I refer also to Oe's indefeasible moral presence and his wrenching fictions, which compel respect.

Yet when Oe writes politically, my mind wanders. And when Karatani does, I breathe deeply and close the book. Though Karatani's prose may bristle with neologisms, I have heard it all before. The question returns: what can the Left really do in Japan when the dregs and dross of Marxism have finally washed out to sea?

The last time I saw Karatani was at a conference on "Represen-
tations of Otherness" in California. He looked jet-lagged, as usual, and
drifted in and out of the building to cop a smoke. A ragtag gang of
intellectual desperadoes lurked about, looking to mug speakers ideo-
logically. Though he may have felt vaguely sympathetic to their politics,
Karatani appeared distant—he had probably never encountered such
coarse antics in Japan, certainly not in the editorial meetings of *Hihyo
Kukan* (*The Space of Criticism*), his magazine. At times he seemed even
forlorn, more sadness in him than bitterness, as if discovering loss.

I thought, beyond the politics of hope or disillusionment, of the ineluctable loss we all feel when we awaken to the "real world." Or
was there another, still more real, world awaiting our second sight? I
copied for Karatani the last poem that a fourteenth-century Zen master, Soseki Muso, wrote:

> In the real world
> the pure world
> no separation exists
> why wait
> for another time
> and another meeting
> the teaching
> on Vulture Peak
> is here today
> who else
> are you looking for
> to preserve the Way?

But I never gave him the poem.

PART III
"THEM"

PRIMARY DIFFERENCES
(SPACE, TIME, PEOPLE)

Though born in Cairo, I feel wholly American—that's America's gift—feel it particularly in Japan. How, then, do I experience the differences between America and Japan, between Iwamoto and myself, friends across mutant genes? Ignoring those relentless gametes, which have shaped our little destinies since humanoid Lucy or mythical Eve, I think of primary differences, human differences, in space, in time, and in that blooded abstraction we call a people.

The Japanese archipelago curves like a ribbed, flying boomerang, serrated on every side by the sea. The country crowds into an area smaller than California. One, a mountainous—71 percent of the land is mountainous—island nation, packed with more than nine hundred people per square mile; the other, a state among fifty, in a continental republic of less than seventy inhabitants per square mile. Numbers have consequences.

Every time I visit Japan, I adjust with a small shudder to the crowds, I who will peevishly cross the street in Milwaukee when I hear someone walking twenty feet behind me. On the Odakyu Line, returning from dinner at the Seiyo Hotel, say, where "tout est luxe, calme, et volupté," I feel that the evening has ended in a polite mauling, a ceremonial battering, more psychic than physical; I feel impacted, driven deep into my body's shell.

The Japanese, of course, take better to imploded space. Once, Japanese friends visited us in Canberra when I held a fellowship there at the Humanities Research Centre. Husband and wife were distinguished intellectuals, sophisticates, fluent in several languages. But they looked around as if they had come to the Outback. We went sightseeing, driving through the wide, deserted avenues radiating from Parliament House. I saw the wife's eyes gradually dilate. Suddenly, she turned to me:

"Do they have much mental sickness here?"

"I really don't know," I answered, puzzled. "What makes you ask?"

She paused, murmured to herself, "It's so empty."

I finally caught on. "Well," I said, "they did some experiments with rats in America, and found that *crowding* increases their hostility, their nuttiness."

She nodded distantly.

In Japan, of course, crowding breeds good manners. Living in close and continual proximity, people must formalize their interactions. Inhabiting a shrinking and permeable space, they shun abrasiveness, cultivate the gestures of sweetness and acquiescence. On some occasions, say in partial undress, they may practice a ritual invisibility and become more inaccessible to one another than two Englishmen sharing a train compartment, each pretending to read his *Times*.

Yeats described Ireland: "Great hatred, little room." In Japan, since the Muromachi period, the "hatred" has found creative outlets, the "little room" abetted miniaturization. Japan excels in doing more with less, turning the edict of dearth into a mandate for production. How different, we say, from the American psychology of sprawl and waste. Yet it was that quintessential American and latter-day Transcendentalist, Buckminster Fuller, who articulated the concept of "ephemeralization": matter dwindles, he said, when mind (design) maximizes energy. Thus, after monstrous ENIAC, which I once glimpsed in the basement of the Moore School of Electrical Engineering I attended, comes the "ephemeral" microchip. Next? A mere silicon shadow or whisper, a new gnosticism.

In Japan, the pressure of imploded space on human intelligence inspires designs of marvelous accuracy and concision. Everywhere, it seems, except in the northern wilderness of Hokkaido, thought expands space into hyperspace. Houses are like a magician's box, turning tricks with double bottoms, secret walls; cars pile in stacks, four or five high in parking lots; private garages below diminutive "mansions" tilt at thirty degrees to accommodate the Mercedes 500 or Rolls Silver Cloud; even refrigerators, the size of a bread box, seem able to swallow a whole case of beer.

The imperatives of space create curious conceits. In Seijo, where we lived for several months, small cabbage plots, midget warehouses, and billionaires' villas (like designer shoeboxes) nestled next to one another. Dubbed the Beverly Hills of Tokyo—Kurosawa, Mifune, Ozawa, Oe, others, reside there—Seijo has the feel of a swank, cramped, calmly sophisticated neighborhood that cannot forget its peasant past. Under the same straw-roofed shed, a blazing-red Porsche may park alongside a rusting tractor, barely an inch between vehicles.

Of course, the Japanese have an advantage, their small statures. Bathtubs, urinals, doors, chairs, beds, fences, shoes, ties, even stamps, it seems, correspond to their size. But the Japanese, I have said, are growing taller; the *shinjinrui* tower above their parents. How many Oedipal quips and tiffs on this topic, I wonder, ensue in Japanese homes.

Space also shapes attitudes to nature, the space of all our spaces. The Japanese claim to revere nature and deface it everywhere the economic imperative prevails. "Nature," then, becomes framed, evoked symbolically, preserved in microcosm: the ikebana in the alcove, the miniature Zen garden by the gate, the bonsai tree in the tokonoma. In other words, "Nature" becomes an allusion to nature, a semiotic reference, a trace of the earth. Or else it becomes an experience, packaged efficiently for zealous groups. What visitor to Japan has not felt outrage and incredulity mingle at the famous sights, in Nikko, Hakone, Kyoto, watching phalanxes of tourists, massed behind their leaders' flags, assault the scenery, urged on by blaring loudspeakers?

To the common or profane eye, space in Japan seems the rarest, the ultimate, commodity. Except in rural regions or a few urban preserves, natural space has become largely denatured. Yet speaking with the Japanese, I often felt that nature remains for them a sacral memory, recalling harmony and plenitude. Call it maternal space.

And time? I was born in an ancient land, its vaunted civilization among the oldest in the world, but I felt no advantage to history there and chose America to escape mummy memories and rhetoric of the blood. In America, I could reshape the past with the future and reinvent time within the limits of my talents and mortality. I did not feel that old was always good.

To the Japanese, though, time is friendliest in repetition, continuity. They derive history from light, from the sun goddess Amaterasu—note the gender of the sun, unusual in myth. They derive all their emperors from her as well, an unbroken line reaching back to the legendary Jimmu-*tenno*, a line that still incarnates the *Yamato kokoro*, the heart or spirit of the originary Yamato people. From temples and cemeteries, from groves and *butsudan* (household shrines), their ancestors call them to unwavering pieties. But traditions constrain as well as sustain. Thus superstitions, atavisms of the quaintest kind, may persist in Japan from generation to generation, insouciant of satellite or supercomputer. Never offer four things as a gift—four flowers, fruits, lacquer bowls—because the sounds for "four" and "death," *shi*, are the same in Japanese.

I lived better in the gaps and cracks of American time; I found in its discontinuities freedom to grow. I could never accept the grip of Japanese custom, the sense of racial predestination. It amounted to a kind of obedience, obedience to circumstance certainly, perhaps even premature obedience to one's death. Yet that same obedience gave the Japanese insane courage in war and freed them to live happily, zestfully, within narrow choices.

Old is good: that's a tilt of temper, marking everywhere the difference between conservative and radical. I am both and neither, a teetering independent, as I like to say, who finds in time past, present, and future both blindness and insight. But I recognized in Japan, in much of Asia, the sacred power of the past. Thus Basho, we saw, bursts silently into tears before the ruins of Taga Castle. Thus, too, three centuries later, Tanizaki extols the dark luster of old Japanese houses.

Yet nowhere is technology more ruthlessly evolved. Thus, Japanese time seems multiple, polychronic, different kinds of time, moving at different speeds on different linear and nonlinear tracks. This is only to say that the Japanese themselves are eclectic, syncretic, pluralist in ideas that leave their identity intact; they take paradox and incongruity in their stride. Why, then, shouldn't Mythic, Shinto, Buddhist, Confucian, Christian, Modern, and PoMo time coexist in the same mental or architectural frame?

And why shouldn't time flow in various tempos? Punctual to a fault—actually, they often arrive a few minutes early—the Japanese can also kill time waiting stoically in line or speed it frantically as, say, a bellboy races to his calls, a golf foursome jogs through eighteen holes. Even the Japanese body seems to obey cycles of its own. Is that why, I jokingly ask Iwamoto, the Japanese age differently from others? He cocks his head and smiles, "Really?"

Time lives in the body, like sex, like death, but it also heeds cultural codes. I can still recall my astonishment on first landing in America, a callow Egyptian college boy, when I saw everyone—dockworkers, immigration officers, taxi drivers—move so slowly. Yet America was the most productive country in the world. I interpreted the deliberate gesture, the leisurely amble, the unhurried speech, as marks of independence, declarations of freedom. No American would run to do another's bidding, as an Egyptian might. In Japan, they ran less from a sense of subordination than of obligation or natural zeal—a determination to excel in all things. In America, time seemed distributed equally among all. The deliberate pace said, "We are all equal." Later, I understood this to be an illusion. Time was money, after all, and money was hardly held in equal shares.

No wonder that American democracy has begun to sour, becoming a democracy of resentments as Tocqueville presaged. Time in Japan was still held in common trust. The rich there knew how to recycle usefully their leisure; the poor received bonuses and holidays; rich and poor believed in the primordial value of work. And they have all amassed now enough time, enough money, to go around, even if the inequities of the *narikin* (new rich) have commenced to grate. Is it, again, the memory of dearth, the sense of a harsher reality, that teaches the Japanese to defer their pleasures, give time its due? Call it exigency of time, call it tolerance for frustration—call it simply patience.

Egyptians, except the long-suffering fellahin, do not defer their pleasures easily. Puritans knew the discipline of deferral, but their descendants have let the discipline fade; the pursuit of happiness means only happiness now. The Japanese endure. In America, we say, "Enjoy now, pay later," and so try to buy everything, including joy, on time. In Japan, they pay first—telephone, travel, shopping cards—and use carefully afterwards. This is another use of time, time saved, time past held in common reverence, trickling out slowly. Why squander it? It will always be there, perdurable, this ancestral time, assuring the Japanese of their identity.

And so it always comes back to people, prime among primary factors, not simply geography or history, or "the system" as some still like to say, but people, the same people who first put me off at Haneda Airport.

Who are the Japanese?

There are two ready answers. The first claims that the Japanese are a perfectly homogeneous people, children all of the goddess Amaterasu. The second denounces the first as a repressive political myth. Put another way, one is a "triumphalist" discourse of the Right, the other a "critical" discourse of the Left, each serving a particular ideology, forever, like Jonathan Swift's Big Enders and Little Enders, forever at odds. Such is the neediness of ideology, its poverty in reality.

Wherever they came from, Asia and the Pacific during the Pleistocene, the Japanese consolidated their rule in western Honshu, the land of Yamato. Their first historical emperor, Jimmu, dates from the seventh century before our era. Today, the old strains (Ainu, Korean, Mongol, Chinese, Malay, Melanesian) have mixed; the Japanese have married and talked themselves— through Nihonjinron (discourse on Japanesehood), kokutai (Japanese essence), Yamato kokoro (Japanese spirit), and other fancy stories of a special destiny—into uniformity. Nearly two and a half centuries of Tokugawa isolation helped.

The Tokugawas founded perhaps the most hierarchic, certainly the most efficient, police state in the premodern world. But before they sealed the country hermetically—only shuinsen (red seal) ships were authorized to sail the high seas—merchants and missionaries came to barter and convert, which sometimes amounted to the same. A powerful Jesuit, Alessandro Valignano, remarked in the sixteenth century on the "Japanese mixture of cruelty, dignity, depravity, and hypocrisy," a mixture so complex, he said, as to defy analysis. A more benign contemporary, an anonymous Englishman, wrote: "The inhabitants shewe a notable witte, and an incredible pacience in sufferinge, labour, and sorrowes. They take greate and diligent care lest, either in worde or deede, they should shewe either feare, or dulnesse of mynde, and lest they should make any man (whosoever he be) partaker of their troubles and wantes. . . . They suffer not the least injurie in the worlde to pass unrevenged." In the meantime, the "inhabitants" portrayed all Westerners with noses worthy of Cyrano or Pinocchio and continued to keep themselves pure.

Pariahs remain in Japan, of course, most notably the buraku-min, "people of the village," once associated with the "unclean" trades of butchers, tanners, gravediggers, now militant untouchables in a postindustrial era. Pariahs remain, and also minorities, from the autochthonous "hairy" Ainus in Hokkaido, through Koreans whose families have lived for several generations in Japan, to Iranians newly arrived in a bizarre barter of oil for work visas, loitering mournfully around Ueno Park. Still, unexceptionably, we may consider the Japanese homogeneous compared to most nations in this hybrid world.

This homogeneity struck me first sitting in the back row of the Kabuki-za. I was waiting for the performance to commence, my eyes wandering idly in expectation of strutting actors, nightmare masks, a riot of hummingbirds disguised as kimonos. Suddenly I saw it before me: a slope of smooth black hair. It was eerie. The back of immobile heads hid the uniqueness of each face. I had never before seen such uniformity in human appearances. It was an anthropological epiphany of sorts, this valley of black hair, marking me inexorably foreign in consciousness—though I, too, had black hair turning gray—marking me as an outsider.

Fiction or fact, then, Japanese "homogeneity," like Japanese "uniqueness"—more on that later—has become a shared assumption, an effective reality, effective even among skeptical outsiders. Traveling through Asia, again and again I find myself noting subliminally the differences between Koreans and Japanese, Chinese and Japanese, Singaporeans and Japanese. Though such comparisons may not always flatter the Children of the Sun, the comparisons tacitly collude with kokutai, the idea of "Japanese national essence."

Kokutai can insinuate itself in strangers as well, becoming a kind of submission. Toward foreign guests, the Japanese are infinitely hospitable; toward outsiders who want to "go native," they are infinitely aloof, not to say hostile. This contrasts sharply with Americans, who believe everyone wants to become American. The Japanese believe no one can ever become Japanese. Hence the fuss about Konishiki, a 576-pound American sumo wrestler, Samoa-born, who won the Emperor's Cup three times.

Though Konishiki speaks Japanese, married a Japanese, has applied for Japanese citizenship, and excels in a quintessentially Japanese ritual-drama-sport, still, in the eyes of many admirers he remains foreign. How, then, can he be elevated to the ultimate rank of *yokozuna*? Can an alien ever possess, beyond skill and strength, the sacred spirit of sumo known as *hinkaku* (gracefulness, subtlety, sophistication)? The controversy rose to a higher pitch when Akebono, a Hawaiian American, did finally ascend to *yokozuna* in 1993, the first non-Japanese ever to be so exalted.

There is a cartoon. A hurrying Japanese bumps accidentally into a tall foreigner and falls down in the street (this would never actually happen to the nimble Japanese). He picks himself up, brushing off his suit. The foreigner apologizes profusely, in perfect, idiomatic Japanese. The Japanese reels backward, falls again, hair standing on end, muttering "Hen na gaijin" (strange/crazy foreigner). This is not only the stuff of cartoons. In *More Like Us*, James Fallows cites a Japanese interpreter who exclaims, "Ah, it gives me the creeps," on hearing an American speak her language like a native.

The inverse phenomenon is no less acute and true. Nothing irritates the Japanese more than a tourist nisei or sansei. Wholly Japanese in appearance, that person nonetheless acts and speaks like a foreigner. What richness of confusion there lies—confusion of roles, histories, identities—what ethnic transvestism, what ancestral impieties. It is like watching your shadow walk away from you, or hearing yourself speak a language you never learned, or seeing your face in the mirror suddenly dissolve into another face.

All people, all cultures, spin around themselves myths of self-regard. In these confirming narratives, assurance never displaces wholly self-doubt. We can not expect the Japanese to call themselves, as the ancient Chinese called them, the people of *Wa*, an ideogram designating, among other things, a dwarf. But we are surprised when they look continually abroad for hints of their own worth. Japanese artists of every kind, especially artists of the avant-garde, must succeed abroad before they receive approval at home. This may be changing now, as the two Hara Museums, in and outside Tokyo, show. But the great Akira Kurosawa still goes begging in Japan. (The usual explanation is that he is too difficult, too arrogant, this Tenno, this Emperor Kurosawa.) The old, fatuous joke about the elephant comes to mind: the Germans want to dissect it scientifically, the French to discover its best culinary parts, the Americans to make money with it in a circus, and the Japanese? They want, of course, to know how it likes Japan. Call it national anxiety, call it national narcissism, it comes across the same.

It is easy to mock the vulnerabilities of the Japanese. Mockery, as Americans should know, can be the other side of envy. Yes, the Japanese miracle of rebirth had its huge human cost, as intellectuals never cease to remind us. Even miracles come with a price tag. The Japanese have risen from atomic ashes to create the world's second-largest economy, growing still, and this merits a salute. They have risen from their self-inflicted desolation, urged by a fierce need to redeem their history, transcend a harrowing defeat. Of this, they rarely used to speak.

Things have now changed. "You won the war, we won the peace," says the grimly impassive Japanese detective to his flamboyant American counterpart in the film Black Rain. This is slick movie talk. But no one who has read Masuji Ibuse's reticent masterpiece, Black Rain (no relation whatever to the later film), about the Hiroshima bomb—indeed, no one who has simply visited the "peace" museums at Hiroshima or Nagasaki, with their silent hordes of Japanese schoolchildren and tourists—can doubt the aching (I almost said festering) presence of the event.

Things are always ambiguous in Japan, though. The power of memory may have rebuilt Japan, shaped its policies and subliminally its people. Still, the young now claim indifference to the war, indifference to the point of numbness. They claim to identify with particular groups, not with Japan as a nation-state. The evidence seems to me more mixed.

Over the last three decades, I have often lectured in Japan on American culture. Sometimes, after a lecture on the Southern novel, some member of the audience would discreetly confide to me his sympathy for the defeated South. The confider was always older, often male. When I broach the question of the war with younger female students, they appear a little puzzled, faintly vague or bored. Perhaps the question is fading into the distractions of affluence, the hopes of a homemade world. But perhaps, too, the question waits to take on a new edge, a new form, among both young and old. Not all rightists in Japan, after all, are aged *kasekijinrui* (fossil breed).

SEIJI TSUTSUMI
(Takashi Tsujii)

I wonder what Seiji Tsutsumi remembers, deep down, of the war.

In his sixties, he remains svelte. Boyish face, a light lisp. The subtle alchemy of his character conceals loneliness, pride, a vulnerability known only to his literary works, written under the pseudonym Takashi Tsujii. Known also, no doubt, to his women.

The alchemy—inherited perhaps from his extraordinary mother, also a poet—conceals other things: resistance, a strain of ruthlessness, an idealism screaming silently to get out. But the obvious shyness and high courtesy of the man are also real, as real, say, as *A Stone Monument on a Fine Day*, a selection of Tsujii's poems, translated into English.

The world knows him, of course, as Seiji Tsutsumi, founding chairman of the Saison Corporation—Seibu Department Stores, Inter-Continental Hotels, Family Mart, Aero Asahi, Saison Insurance, etc.—a multi-billion-dollar empire. Knows him as a dazzling, daring marketer, no, the seer of a generation, intuiting both the material and immaterial needs of the young. As James Sterngold put it in *The New York Times*, "Saison, in fact, has helped define a new generation of restless consumers searching, with their wallets full of yen, for the image of soulfulness and individuality that Mr. Tsutsumi has projected onto his companies."

I know him otherwise, as a host, as a writer, perhaps the most elusive of my acquaintances. His intricate shyness and courtesy struck me first. Once he unwrapped a small present Sally and I offered him, unwrapped it with feline grace, discreetly slipping ribbon and tape into his coat pocket. Another time, he stood at the doorstep of his white, spare mansion in Minami-Azabu, to see us off, after lunch, in one of his chauffeured limousines. He does this with all his guests. But on that day, I remarked his half-averted face, waiting for the car to pull out— that awkward, interminable moment after all the farewells have been said—remarked some shadow of long-ago pain. I looked away.

Make no mistake: the man is not fragile. He has held by the force of his hermetic personality a constellation of businesses that may explode any time into financial chaos or implode into a black hole of debts. Neither possibility is likely: Tsutsumi has worked hard to create an information network, a noetic force, that holds his world together like gravity itself.

This is achievement enough. But I wonder about the mind, once nurtured on Marxism and Surrealism, that writes in "The Age of Disturbance":

> When one bit into a red apple
> the disturbance shone out clearly—fire in a distant village;
> and around the tumble-down castle
> a pastel-colored wind blew.

Or writes in the preface to the same selection of poems: "Now, in the last years of the 20th century, the great question is, where is the world heading? But even as they keep so momentous a question in mind, poets who are living now must also take into their hearts small matters such as no political and social leader would take heed of, and they must do so, not out of any secular interests, but out of spiritual concerns, which have to do with the beauty, sadness, and loneliness of humanity."

Perhaps that, more than any other, is the concern of Tsujii through all his volumes of poetry, fiction, essays. Perhaps it is the elimination of "rust," an act of spiritual purification dear to the Japanese, in *In a Time of Rust*. Perhaps it is a child's and man's reckoning with his looming family—powerful father, mother pliant like steel, driving sister and half-brothers, one, Yoshiaki Tsutsumi, reputed the richest man in the world—as in the autobiographical novel, *A Spring Like Any Other*. Or perhaps, after all, it is the invisible legacy of the war, of Japan itself, that remains his unacknowledged burden.

Though immensely traveled, Tsutsumi is at home only in his own language—a writer's gift, after all—ambivalently at home only in his own culture. He does not rush back to Tokyo to eat sushi, as some traveling Japanese executives do; he finds that foreign cities "provide much more fuel for the imagination," as he says in an interview. At the same time, he likes "the mess of Tokyo...that part of it which is not logically consistent." Likes Okinawa, too, "where you can still get a sense of the Asia that Japan is part of." And likes, I suspect, the sereness, the rust in its other *sabi* sense, the *mono no aware* or pathos of Japanese existence.

Tsutsumi: yes, opaque, oblique, changeful, and no doubt tyrannical where excellence demands it—an asymmetrical nature. But also, beyond all complexities, candid where it counts, lucid. I have not met many Japanese, in high or low places, who would admit:

> My companies progressively employ more Koreans and Chinese and Burakumin. But discrimination in Japan is very deep and people use delicate words to camouflage wrong attitudes. Perhaps it's because this is a small island. Still, we have to let our people become accustomed to living and working with other tribes and races. In our companies I hope that we are helping to start that mix. It is so necessary for our society....
>
> I'm always trying to better the position of women in my companies, but it is very difficult. Men are very jealous, even under the guise of being protective. I have to use fifty to sixty times more energy to make a woman an executive than to make a man one. Still, women are gradually increasing their power and position in all my companies.

But then, I have not met many American businessmen who can refer accurately in the course of an interview to Adam Smith, Marx, Weber, Adorno, Derrida, Yanagita Kunio, Motoori Norinaga—and win the Faulkner or Pulitzer (as Tsujii won the Tanizaki) Prize. Nor have I met many who can put to such creative use their own personal, invincible alienation.

EXCEPTIONALISM

W. H. Auden hit the dragon's eye when he perceived that the "error bred in the bone" is to be "loved alone." This is ME, an ontic cry, a wail as loud as the Fall. But there are also collective forms of "the error bred in the bone": for instance, ideas of national exceptionalism.

Already, in the sixteenth century, Valignano noted with exasperation that the Japanese "deliberately try to be unlike other people." This need seems to persist in the Japanese: they still perceive themselves as exceptional, "not in the way that all cultures are unique," Karel van Wolferen says in *The Enigma of Japanese Power*, "but somehow uniquely unique, ultimately different from all others." Indeed, myths of exceptionalism vary, vary even in their contradictions, often their most revealing parts. I recall Egyptian as well as American versions of such myths.

Throughout my childhood in Egypt, I heard the Song of Time: how the Pharaohs ruled the known world, how their civilization preceded, exceeded, all others—look at temple, obelisque, pyramid, and tomb, are they not awesome, even in ruin? They are awesome indeed, though few Egyptians could claim their builders as ancestors. The uniqueness of Egypt was that, lying at the crossroads of the world and time, it was so often overrun, maintaining still over the millennia a peerless continuity of estival rhythms and human miseries. Perhaps, after all, that was the paradox of uniqueness.

And America? Columbus did not discover the passage to India; he discovered a place, a myth really, of complete alterity, strange men and birds and beasts, gold hills in a landscape of dreams— a place exotic, like Japan a century later. But the early conquistadores who followed him may have had other, more obscure motives in their hearts. William Carlos Williams put it thus in In the American Grain: "They moved out across the seas stirred by instincts, ancient beyond thought as the depths they were crossing, which they obeyed under the names of King or Christ. . . . At the back, as it remains, it was the evil of the whole world; it was the perennial disappointment which follows, like smoke, the bursting of ideas."

Something here evokes the motive of America's uniqueness, which became a Puritan myth, deriving directly from God's Grace. This myth promised the New Jerusalem, the White City on the Hill, redemption from History. Later, in the more secular moment of the American Revolution, the myth assumed the fulfillment of the European Enlightenment, creating a society dedicated to life, liberty, and the pursuit of happiness. Then the frontier opened, the extravagant West. This heralded a Manifest Destiny for America, also called imperialism, extending beyond the Rockies, beyond the Pacific even. The familiar words of Commodore Perry still resound, echoing with ironies in our ears: "Westward will the course of empire take its way. . . . The people of America will, in some form or other, extend their dominion and their power until they shall have brought within their mighty embrace multitudes of the Islands of the great Pacific, and placed the Saxon race upon the eastern shores of Asia."

The "Saxon race" found its way to Hawaii, Guam, Wake, and

the Philippines, but already in America it was superseded by immigrants of other "races" and their American Dream, which offered still another version of uniqueness. That dream of oppor-
tunity persisted, mixed with earlier versions, through America's
high moment after the Second World War, as the premier superpower in the world. The land of immigrants and God's own
country, we see, achieved its exceptional destiny, not by exclusion
but inclusion, not in serene consensus but in abrasive conflict,
not by feudal valor, but by technological prowess. What form the
myth of America's uniqueness now takes in this postmodern
world is harder to discern. But here is Baudrillard in *America:*

> Today, America no longer has the same hegemony, no longer
> enjoys the same monopoly, but it is, in a sense, uncontested
> and uncontestable. It used to be a world power, it has now
> become a model (business, the market, free enterprise, per-
> formance)—and a universal one—even reaching as far as
> China. The international style is now American. There is no
> real opposition any more; the combative periphery has now
> been reabsorbed (China, Cuba, Vietnam); the great anti-
> capitalist ideology has been emptied of its substance. All in
> all, the same consensus is forming around the US in the
> world at large as has developed around Reagan at home.

In a striking paradox, Baudrillard seems to claim that the
uniqueness of America now rests on the fact that it is no longer
unique; it has become, rather, a model, an immanent style, a
shared, uncontested vision. In any case, it is no longer unique
for precisely the same reason that Japan, to the degree that it
succeeds as a superpower, must cease to be unique. In this scenario, we have all become "a case among cases," as Clifford
Geertz puts it, contemplating our hybrid, interactive world.

Is the scenario very different in Japan? The Japanese do not consider themselves God's chosen people, because they acknowledge no single, paramount deity. Their identity is more mythical, more tribal, than theological.

The myth persists today in ways both trivial and grave. It may explain, for instance, the earlier paucity of Japanese ethnography as a proud indifference to the world. It may account for those old signs at Narita Airport reading "Aliens," suggesting extraterrestrial visitors going through passport control, and for the current surveys showing that more than 60 percent of the Japanese would prefer to have no contact whatsoever with foreigners. It may derive from the unbroken line of emperors, reverting to the Sun. (That myth, incidentally, coincides with the moment of Westernization in the Meiji Period and differs considerably from ancestor myths in older chronicles, the Kojiki, say, or the Nihonki.) The myth may boast the fact that Japan was not conquered prior to 1945, not even by the Golden Horde of the Great Khan. It may account for the practice of fingerprinting all resident aliens, even third- or fourth-generation Koreans, indistinguishable often from the Japanese. It may find daily proof in the Japanese language, its grammar, diction, syntax, and all its three scripts, kanji, katakana, and hiragana. Finally, it may adduce the grisliest of events, atomic destruction, as evidence of a unique fate.

But Japanese exceptionalism, like all kinds of exceptionalism—that of Israel, for instance—can be a plea for special treatment. Then exceptionalism, transcending the human community, invokes supramoral rights. Exceptionalism can also take ludicrous as well as baneful forms. Thus, for instance, we hear that Japanese snow is different from other snow, that the Japanese brain encodes certain sounds differently from other brains (the actual experiments suggest more nuance) that American electric currents are not "friendly" to Japanese computers, and that—as a former cabinet minister said—the Japanese cannot consume

much American beef because their intestines are longer than anyone else's. These opinions are not altogether harmless. As Clyde
Haberman put it, "The lack of kinship the Japanese feel toward
the rest of the world can mask an element of amorality." This
is the amorality of ancient tribalism as well as modern nationalism.

The myth of Japanese uniqueness, however, is far more complex than Japanese isolation, racism, or xenophobia would suggest. For the myth rests on contradictory ideas of uniqueness,
which often contains its own anxieties. Thus Japan's insistence
on its distinctiveness may also betray its old identity problem,
reverting to massive borrowings from China in the seventh century, continuing through massive appropriations from the West
during the Meiji Restoration. The paradoxes persist. For instance,
while Herman Kahn speaks of Japan as the emergent superstate
and Ezra Vogel calls it Number One, Kitaro Nishida, in his history of *mu no basho*, sees it as the "topos of nothingness," a kind
of praise; and closer to our time, in despair of its vacuous modernization, Yoshimi Takeuchi says, "Japan is nothing."

The signal word here that provides the clue to Japan's both
unique and shared fate is the word *modernization*. Since the Meiji
Revolution in 1868, from the writings of Yukichi Fukuzawa,
through the prewar Co-Prosperity Sphere, the wartime Kyoto
Symposium (1942), and the postwar Hakone Conference
(1960), to our own *posutomodanizumu*, the question of modernization has haunted Japanese self-awareness. What, exactly, is this
modernization? Theodore von Laue put it thus: "[Japan's achievement since 1945] represents the most startling triumph of the
world revolution of Westernization: a non-Western country signally successful in terms of Western achievements." This statement, though lacking in nuance, underscores the real point:
namely, Japan's vaunted doubleness, at once Asian and Western,

both itself and another. This is a different form of uniqueness, then, a postmodern form, double coded, uninterested in "purity." Or, to paraphrase the great architect Arata Isozaki, "I work in mental equidistance from Kyoto's Katsura Detached Palace and the Greek Parthenon."

Thus, we see in both America and Japan, not to mention in Egypt, that myths of exceptionalism bristle with contrarieties; the self is already infected by the other, the other by the self. This, I think, is salubrious, salutary, for contamination can be a kind of enrichment, two systems in complicity, if not symbiosis. Such complicity enables transcultural discourse.

Or does it? Here, perhaps, a touch of irony, a touch of realism, may set the record of transculturalism straighter. James Fallows quotes an exasperated American diplomat thus:

> Let's be like Japan! First we rig politics so that one party is always in power and big-city votes basically don't count. Then we double the cost of everything but hold incomes the same. Then we close the borders and start celebrating racial purity. Then we reduce the number of jobs for women. . . . Then we set up a school system that teaches people not to ask questions. After a while we can have a trade surplus too.

SHUICHI KATO

Who could be more exceptional or less given to myths of exceptionalism?

They call him sometimes, Americans do, the Edmund Wilson of Japan. It is a misnomer. True, Kato—no one addresses him as Shuichi, not even his wife, Midori—is a prolific polymath, fluent in English, French, German, Italian, Chinese; his collected works, now fifteen volumes and growing, range magisterially over the cultures of East and West. But Kato trained as a physician, a hematologist, and his sensibility lacks the kinks and crotchets of the great American critic.

In 1945, Kato investigated, with a U.S.-Japan joint medical team, the effects of the atomic bomb on Hiroshima. What does a Japanese, twenty-six years old at the time, think when he sees twisted steel, burnt skin, bleached blood, fire in the bone? Kato, whatever he thought, looked with steady gaze. Later, he wrote, with Robert Jay Lifton and Michael Reich, *Six Lives/Six Deaths: Portraits from Modern Japan*, not about atomic blight but the ultimate lucidity of death.

We shared across the Pacific a student, Kit Pancoast, who introduced us in a triangular correspondence. Our appointment was at the Tokyo International House in Roppongi. He came toward me in rapid, shuffling steps, a small man with leonine head and large, attentive eyes. He did not smile, except with his eyes, which evoked in me those "ancient, glittering eyes" of Yeats's "Lapis Lazuli."

Kato reads a little from the Chinese classics every day; he will not read, he once told me, any prose less accomplished than his own. Japanese critics agree: his austere prose finds a match only in Jun Ishikawa and the Meiji physician Ogai Mori, another polymath. In all their prose, one senses what no translation can obscure—that steely edge of mind that makes for true style, a mode of awareness or being, a life on the line.

But Kato possesses what Mori lacked: resistance, opposition to the Japanese Way when opposition is due. In his monumental A History of Japanese Literature, he wrote, "The society which has developed since the end of the war is one which is insensitive to the human rights and the opinions of minority groups.... The Japanese indigenous world-view is basically sublunary and contains no transcendent values." Once, barely smiling, he advised me to refuse the "easy beguilements of our exotic culture." He said it with irony but also with a certain gusto, reminding me of yet another polymath, Kenneth Burke, who counseled, "When in Rome, do as the Greeks do."

I quickly recognized in Kato this capacity for dissent, rare in his obedient society. "We are a sensuous, not an intellectual culture," he once said to me, "and this discourages radical thought." He paused. "I don't mean radical in politics only." Then somberly: "But it's also true, we have become politically apathetic." Perhaps Kato recalled the activism of earlier postwar decades; probably he disliked, with a touch of indulgence, the new consumerism in Japan; certainly he distrusted what he called "our latest fashion, GNP nationalism."

Still, without a tinge of chauvinism, Kato remains wholly at ease in his own tradition, which he knows "by heart." In slow, accented rhythms, he will discourse as happily on Basho, Hinayana Buddhism, Albigensian heresies, French Impressionism, or the origins of Thanksgiving. His large eyes brighten, a hint puckish; he may even toss back his white mane and laugh. That's what he did, one evening at his house, when Midori-san—herself, as Midori Yajima, a versatile intellectual and critic of Italian film—surprised us with a turkey at dinner. It happened to be Thanksgiving in Tokyo, and we had forgotten it.

August fair-mindedness, a rare ability for self-criticism, a knack for the larger view in contemplating even the smallest thing—such qualities would be sufficient to distinguish him in any Japanese academic milieu. Kato has indeed taught at major universities in Japan, the United States, Canada, Britain, Switzerland, Italy, Germany, France, and I, like others, address him as Professor Kato or Kato *sensei*. But he remains supra-academic. His life is ampler, its deepest perceptions catholic, if not universal. That may be why, in his introduction to Kato's *The Japan-China Phenomenon*, Arnold Toynbee wrote, "Mr. Kato's acute observations do not date." Time abhors our narrower loyalties.

STEREOTYPES AND PARADOXES
(COOLNESS, COURTESY, CONFORMITY)

Two-handed and double-brained, human beings understand by comparisons, similitudes, differences, by simplifications also, which lead to stereotypes. These fix reality long enough to grasp and fuss. Then life moves on, leaving us holding a stone block. We understand by contradictions, too, and may perceive paradoxes, or at least incongruities, where an angel may see only seamless reality. Above all, we understand by identification, which may include rejection or projection. In truth, pure empathy is rare. More often, we simply rush to formulate so that we may judge; we may not understand at all.

My mind, especially in youth, favored lyrical abstractions; it may have become more narrative over the years. Though cousin to the desert, I looked on creation with Emersonian, with Swedenborgian, eyes; the *mysterium tremendum et fascinans* lay a hairbreadth beneath all things, ineluctable, forever elusive. Later, I understood more paradoxically—forget dialectics—and from Japan learned to trust surfaces; or rather, I began to learn when and when not to trust them. I saw how stereotypes could dissolve into paradoxes, which aspired to the condition of insight. The insights may curve back on themselves, revealing more of the perceiver than the perceived—this book, I have admitted, is autobiography. Still, stereotypes and paradoxes together can reveal something of a culture at the seams of its contradictions.

The culture of the chrysanthemum and the sword—of courtesy and cruelty, sentimentality and sadism, benign streets and mean pornography—regales us with contradictions. These may arise, as Ruth Benedict has suggested, from the enormous tensions in Japan between a secure, indulgent childhood, on the one hand, and a rigorous, constrained adulthood, on the other. Whatever the cause, I offer here three sets of stereotypes, shading into paradox, as a window, a little glazed, on that distant land.

The Japanese are the most impassive, formal, enigmatic people on earth, more inscrutable than Easter Island monoliths, more distant than those ancient Egyptian statues that looked at me askance throughout my childhood. (Oh, how I longed for a touch of Pharaonic or Japanese aloofness in my own effusive, squabbling Cairene milieu.)

"Distant, inscrutable?" a Japanese friend said to me in genuine puzzlement behind her composed face. "We are, of course, formal in certain situations, but we think of ourselves as very warm." She hesitated. "Forgive me, but we think of westerners as a little too logical and cold, perhaps a little too . . . 'dry.' " Former Prime Minister Yasuhiro Nakasone bears her out: the Japanese, he said, are "monsoon people," and their "wetness" proves their warm, emotional side. (When I read this, I thought of the seven typhoons that Sally and I endured in the fall of 1991, sheets of tepid, unremitting rain, everything in the house dank, the towels forever clammy, sugar and salt caking into white, friable blocks, bamboo sprouting darkly everywhere, shooting up before our eyes—and the smooth, brown gloss on Japanese complexions, glistening with health.)

"Dry" (aloof, ungiving) and "wet" (sentimental, pliant): You can almost hear Margaret Thatcher scolding her cabinet, though in Japan an excess of either signals a fault. But other, cognate polarities come to mind. Anyone who has seen a samurai movie knows the two sides: one ceremonial, choreographic, rigid sometimes, the other chaotic, clownish, even berserk. Or seen a sumo match: two quarter-ton behemoths squaring off, glaring, glowering, fire and ice, taking at most a menacing half step toward one another, all their fury and scorn held back in cascading waves of muscle and fat before exploding in a mayhem of shoves and slaps; then it's over, they bow, sip water ritually, waddle off like hippos puffing their way peacefully to a pond. Stoicism and violence, delicacy and ferocity, live side by side—in fact, live within one another. Again, the chrysanthemum and the sword, suggesting feminine and masculine mystiques, seem always in one culture, if not one soul, compact.

Writers have also found in these rhythms of restraint and recklessness a counterpoint of submission and domination, which may explain Japanese behavior in the Pacific war, their readiness to commit seppuku (ritual suicide), their implacable assaults in kendo—once out of its scabbard, Japanese tradition holds, the sword must go on killing—and their cruelty in prison camps. "The rudest and most violent Japanese god, Susanowo-no-mikoto, wails when his father entrusts him with command over the sea: he desires nothing else but to go to the netherworld in which his deceased mother dwells," writes Kurt Singer in *Mirror, Sword, and Jewel*. And indeed, for Singer, the mother shapes all the secret rhythms of the Japanese heart; "all these signs of passionate passivity in an eager, ambitious people" redound upon her boundless, unconditional love.

Still, the enigma of a teasing calm remains with every visitor to Japan, prompting him to wonder what lies behind the mask?

I wondered, I asked, I refused to accept for answer the fashionable wisdom: Nothing! Yes, there is a deep blandness in Japanese society, a quality of dreamlike ease and flow, as Lafcadio Hearn was among the first to note. Yes, there is little play, irony, contradiction in Japanese conversation, little evidence of what John Donne or Samuel Johnson would call wit. Yes, intellectual life (especially academic life) suffers from a kind of genial imbecility, a lack of tensity, dialectic, introspection, surprise, suffers from a polite disdain not only of logic or abstraction but of ideas themselves. Yes, yes, the Japanese often seem, well, not exactly vacuous, say naive. Donald Richie catches that nuance in his enchanting book, The Inland Sea: "The Japanese always think us younger than we are. That is because they are all so young. The reason they are so young is that they have no conscience, maybe, certainly that there is no cynicism and no corollary of disillusion. No one ever taught them to expect more of life than life can in fact offer. Appearances are reality, the mask is literally the face, and the cynic can find no telltale gap because none exists."

One sunny, spring day, Sally and I had lunch with Richie at the Press Club, top of the Denki Building, overlooking the Outer Imperial Gardens, the Hibiya Crossing, Yurakucho, and the Ginza. Light from a soft, opalescent sky suffuses the dining room as I bring up again the question of Japanese innocence.

"You see," Donald says, "they lack the inwardness of guilt, Judeo-Christian guilt. And they have this idea of sincerity, which repels. . . ."

"Cynicism?" I anticipate.

"Not only cynicism. Repels irony, too, the sense of incongruity."

"So where does all this subtlety come from?" Sally asks.

I break in again: "Crowding? Sensitivity to others?"

"And hierarchy!" both Sally and Donald add.

I could assent to all these observations, all this smug badinage. Still, nothing really behind the mask? Then I recalled the Japanese readiness to sleep in public places, just close the eyes and "meditate"—how exquisitely Japanese that ambiguity of sleep/meditation—shut out the world, drop off, chin to chest, the face going slack. I recalled all the times I entered a subway car on a long suburban ride home and imagined I had entered a moving morgue. I recalled an elegant Japanese couple, next to us at the legendary Taillevent restaurant in Paris, the man dozing upright in his banquette at dinner, perhaps suddenly bushwhacked by jet lag. And I recalled lecture audiences across Japan in which people, even my hosts, would close their eyes, the better to "concentrate."

Naps, of course, may be one of the few permissible forms of withdrawal from the perpetual demands of work, the ubiquitous and insistent claims of sociality, in Japan. But sleep rarely transforms the sleeper into an aesthetic object. The body becomes lumpier, more discombobulated, becomes, for a Westerner at least, a momentary memento mori. Bodies and their functions, though, are never very private in Japan anyway. And these harassed votaries of Morpheus fully deserved their instant of peace. Was it fair to conclude that, awake or asleep, the Japanese concealed from the world blank minds?

True, the Japanese avoid displays of individual virtuosity, forensic skill, flamboyant assertiveness; they detest the willful disregard for custom, which they also interpret as cosmic violence. Stoical as if by second, by acquired, nature, the Japanese seem enigmatic only because their culture exerts intricate and powerful controls, channeling the passions into secret labyrinths, a warren of conduits. But the passions will out! They issue in Japanese myth, art, Bushido, pornography, education, technology, commerce, manners, in everything the Japanese do superlatively, often courteously, sometimes cruelly, well.

The Japanese are the most courteous people in the world—among them, a foreigner can never be too polite, the tourist guidebooks say. Witness the bowing in all its exquisite degrees, the delicate locutions of language, the rituals of self-deprecation, the calibrated exchanges of gifts, above all, the genius for avoiding embarrassment, to others first, to oneself next. Even the captain of a common ferryboat stands at the bottom of the gangplank at journey's end to bow all his passengers to shore. Even the chairman of an academic department, as host, will stand before your hotel door, spiffing up his car with a feather duster before driving you off to a lecture.

"The most courteous?" said my friend, Hisao Kanaseki, a poet-critic, feigning puzzlement. "Oh, you mean the most hypocritical." Paul Theroux, with his usual bad grace, seems to agree; he remarks somewhere that "the Japanese have perfected good manners and made them indistinguishable from rudeness."

Quips, I think, though I know that the Japanese can drive a sharp elbow in the ribs, or hog the "Silver Seats," designated for the aged and invalid, on suffocatingly crowded trains. Nor are those growling daimyos, snarling samurai, murderous peasants, all crouching lust and bellicose energy, only figments of Akira Kurosawa's imagination. Nor does the record of Japanese atrocities in Asia establish them as gentlemen at war.

"Courtesy," said a young Japanese writer to me. "For us, it is survival, a sociobiological imperative; for you Americans it may be a kind of generosity, at worst, a form of sentimentality deriving from a 'nice' view of the world. We can't afford that view." And for Egyptians, now dim in my aging recollection, what is courtesy? A little of both and neither? An erosion of spirit and history? A type of carelessness or fatalism finally?

What lies behind these Japanese images of courtesy or cruelty? Culture, of course, landscape, the subtle interactions of people, nature, and codes, the thick dust of time. Crowded on their jagged islands, living at the edge of dearth, they do what they can to avoid violence to one another and avoid shame. In the end, though, Japanese courtesy strikes the Westerner as almost gratuitous, an aesthetic construct, eluding practical explanations, eluding even moral judgments. Sometimes, it may even seem a touch humorous in its excess. A Japanese colleague once saw me start to wipe my eyeglasses; he took them gently from my hand, sprayed them with a special fluid, and wiped them immaculate with three different types of tissue before returning them to me with a bow.

Two apple stories may give the idea of Japanese courtesy richer nuance.

Once in Toyama, on the Sea of Japan, Sally inquired of her dinner companion about the district's famous apples. She had heard they were delicious. Was it the cool weather that gave them their tang? The man mumbled something noncommittally, and the dinner conversation proceeded at the usual snail's pace. At the end, as everyone was saying goodnight, the man produced mysteriously a beautiful paper bag. With many apologies, he offered it to Sally. It was full of glowing Toyama apples, which, unseen even by Sally, he had phoned his wife to bring. One of the apples had been peeled, dipped in salt water to hold its whiteness, sliced in precisely wedged pieces, provided with decorated toothpicks, and wrapped with its paper plate in cellophane.

Another time, in Tokyo, after a long night of food and drink, Hisao Kanaseki invited us three weeks hence, together with the gifted novelist Natsuki Ikezawa, to his house in order to "continue our various conversations." We were to bring wine and salad; Ikezawa-san, who had recently won the Akutagawa Prize—soon he was to win the Tanizaki as well—promised something delectable and mysterious. A new manuscript, I asked? He laughed, waving his palm rapidly, vertically, waving his hand from side to side in front of his face: No. Two weeks passed without the promised confirmation of time. I decided to call Hisao and beat around the bush—a Japanese would have dropped the matter entirely. It was 9:30 in the morning when I called and Hisao was for a few moments vague, mystified. Then he caught on. Of course, he said, all the arrangements had been made. Forget the salad, forget the wine. Please come at 6:30 P.M. Is the time alright? Half an hour later, Hisao surprised us by appearing at our doorstep—he also lived in Seijo, a ten-minute walk from our house—with a bag of giant apples. He wanted to apologize for being slow on the uptake over the phone. He had been working very late the night before, was scarcely awake when I called. Please excuse my vagueness over the phone, please accept these poor apples. What neither of us would ever admit is that he had forgotten our dinner date. In effect, Hisao's act had erased his lapse, our silence making the erasure permanent.

Is that redemptive courtesy? Perhaps. But there is an aspect of it that is almost disinterested, like poetry say, or like aesthetic sacrifice.

The Japanese are the most cohesive, conformist, tribal, well, yes, racist people around. They are also the most loyal. Like a circular coral reef, like a silvery school of sardines, in stillness as in motion, they adhere. You know the joke: how do you make all Japanese passengers on a sinking ship jump into the sea? You tell them that everyone else has already jumped overboard. But it is

not really a joke. Once at an exclusive restaurant, frequented by
top industrialists and politicians, the headwaiter delicately asked
me to order what the rest of a table of six had ordered, a version of chateaubriand, for the sake of "harmony." Harmony
means the *same*, or nearly the same: until very recently, kimonos
came only in two sizes, for men and for women.

Why, how, vary? From childhood on, the Japanese have heard
a slogan hammered into their heads: "The nail that sticks out
gets hammered down." They shun or harass children who return after studying abroad, *kikoku shijo*, because they have been
"contaminated." One Japanese girl, I recall, who spent her childhood in Cairo with her foreign-service parents, suffered the bizarre moniker "B-17" on returning to Japanese schools. She had
become an alien, a threat from the sky. The threat takes other
forms. Even former Prime Minister Miyazawa meets disapprobation of his fluency in English. Even the future Empress of Japan,
Harvard and Oxford educated, carries the taint of foreignness.

Ah, but these are old tales. Do we not all share them in various measure, in our own sweaty solidarities of the cave, in our
own viscosities of familial life? Perhaps that is why, an outsider,
I always feel in Japan wickedly free, slipping past countless obligations, encrusted nowhere—feel sometimes like a bandit or
outlaw in the land of the *sarariiman* (salaryman).

Loyalty, conformity, homogeneity, the sense of a special common fate: these are what bring the Japanese through, through
dearth, civil wars, cataclysms of every kind, Hiroshima and Nagasaki, the only occupation they ever suffered, current geopolitical rivalries. The conformity may go back to village life, the immemorial, grueling, communal labor in rice fields, a labor now
transplanted to factory floors. (Paradoxically, despite their profound commonality, the Japanese resist touching one another,
preferring a bow to a handshake; they wince at a backslap,

freeze at a cheek kiss, gasp at a hug.) It is also, as conformities go, intricate, permitting acute internal rivalries (see later, under Rivalry). In the end, their circles of loyalty and intimacy remain almost concentric, with some overlapping margins. The center is the *uchi*, the home. With threatening outsiders, *yosomono*, they become progressively formal, rude, finally cruel—that may be why, in restaurants, they unexpectedly prefer private cubicles to the large, bright, noisy, areas that the Chinese or Italians would adore.

Still, isn't it a cheery sight to look out your window, at an ANA plane about to take off, and see all the mechanics, baggage handlers, ground agents, lined up smartly on the tarmac, waving goodbye to all the passengers?

But there's more to these stereotypes. Once, weary of taking off and putting on my shoes ten times that day, I wondered: why do the Japanese really leave their shoes behind on entering a house? Chinese, Arabs, Europeans don't. The Japanese, impeccably clean, claim it to be a self-evident matter of hygiene. I think it may be a sacral matter: the doorstep is liminal, a boundary between sacred space within, profane outside. (The house is an extension of the bed, not the street—house and bed share the same Japanese character.) It is the *uchi* principle again, and a guest will take off his shoes because, so long as he or she remains a guest, the visitor becomes part of the sacred order within: Us, not Them. Hence the powerful appeal of one's village or country origin, the near-mystic *furusato* longing.

Not that the Japanese are wholly spiritual. Shinto birth, Christian marriage, Buddhist burial, pragmatism and technology all around. Their solidarity, in any case, is both mythic and practical; others call it primitive. Primitive? This land of bullet trains, high-definition television, industrial robots, superconductors, and microchips *sans pareil*? Well, yes, in a sense. So many Japanese customs are superstitions sanctioned by time, so many traditions—about birth, marriage, food (especially rice), gifts, ancestors—show their animist heritage. Palm readers beguile "office ladies" on the Ginza streets; shavings of gold floating in miso soup augur longevity, as do long noodles and long-necked cranes; and the harvest god, Inari, still commands sizable followings even in cities.

Even Japanese fads have something primal in them. A bauble from Tiffany, a Vuitton bag, a Harley-Davidson Hog, what to give on Valentine's Day, where to go on a Christmas dinner date—all these seem traces of ancient collective rituals. In this superconsumer society, fashions become instant rite. The demands of style among the trendy, the urge of the *narikin* for display, cannot alone explain the insatiable need for brand names. Each name— Dior, Mercedes, Ralph Lauren—seems like a tribal avatar assuming each day a new form. And in a recession, the fashionable brand names become a label called No Brand Name, sold at Seibu!

Do I exaggerate? The eminent Japanese poet and cultural critic, Makoto Ooka, would not think so. In an essay called "Sitting in a Circle," he suggests that wheel-sitting, or *kurumaza*, is a profound metaphor of Japan itself. A *kurumaza*, of course, excludes others; it also acts as "a formation in which the members constantly keep watch over one another to make sure there are no defectors or dropouts." Ooka speculates that "the rising tension between the United States and Japan ultimately has its roots in the fundamental gap between *kurumaza* and non-*kurumaza* societies." His speculation takes a darker, self-critical turn in these further words: "The same people who are so generous and mutually supportive within the circle are liable to turn into frightfully difficult, arrogant, cruel, and intolerant individuals when dealing with outsiders. What particularly scares and alarms me is that I realize that I share this same tendency." Fortunately for us all, rich people don't fight fanatically—so common wisdom claims.

There is a further twist to this theme: blind circles beget *amae*, dependence. The structure of vassalage, the "anatomy of dependence," as Takeo Doi called it in his famous work by that name, are evident everywhere in Japanese society. Parent and child, teacher and student, senior and junior, *oyabun* and *kobun* (patron and client), perpetuate that dependence in all the broadways and byways of cultural life. Moreover, both *giri* and *ninjo*— traditional Japanese ethical concepts that may be roughly translated as social obligation and human feeling—"have their roots deep in *amae*," Doi argues. Journalists have even extrapolated *amae* to international relations, notably the relation of Japan to the United States. Thus, Masakatsu Horino writes, "Largely due to America's military power, economic success and humane behavior as a victorious occupier, many postwar Japanese perceived their relationship with America in terms of *amae no kankei*, which means 'to depend on another's care and indulge in another's kindness.' . . . This was not so for the emerging majority of younger Japanese, who never experienced postwar hardship or the basis for the *amae* relationship."

Nor do the majority of younger Japanese sit as readily or as often on the floor. Have they severed, then, their relation to the earth? I should be surprised. Despite the Tokyo Tower and the skyscrapers of Shinjuku, so much of Japanese life remains close to the ground—lateral structures, as in the Bunraku stage, predominate. The Japanese bow, sit on tatami mats, sleep on futons, often eat kneeling or with legs crossed at low tables, write sometimes at special desks, their feet dangling in a cavity below the floor. In the spare, elegant houses, rarely higher than two stories, doorways and ceilings are low. The whole center of gravity in Japan seems near the earth. Is this a practical measure against perpetual tremors, shattering earthquakes? Or is it some sort of Antean complex? A refusal of transcendence?

I speak with some envy: I have never felt comfortable barefoot, sitting or sleeping on the ground. My sign is air; I aspire to fire; I would rather have my ashes scattered in the sky than buried in the earth. Does it all come from old disaffections with a mother? The Japanese, however airy or subtle, and however patriarchic since the Kamakura or Warrior Age, belong to mother earth; they are autochthonal. Nature, despite its cataclysms, soothes, nourishes, inspires; Japanese society simply extends nature into history. The primeval mythic community blurs *physis* and *nomos*. With prewar Japan mainly in mind, Singer argues in *Mirror, Sword, and Jewel* that this primordial blurring, if not unity, is the reason for that country's extraordinary durability, a durability akin to nature's.

Well, I understand Singer, though I view his Germanic cultural organicism askance; I, too, have heard the Japanese descant on nature. But I have also seen how the Japanese used nature in the postwar years: driftnet fishing, mercury poisoning, yellow smogs, industrial landscapes out of *Soylent Green*. Will the Japanese, after all, remain the most cohesive, conformist, "earthy" people on this interactive planet? What will happen to the delicate fabric of obligations and abnegations, the vast lacework of interdebtedness, the aesthetics of sacrifice, when an entirely new generation comes of age?

PHOTO ESSAY

HISTORY ANDS ITS FORMS:
(DIS)CONTINUITIES

Miyajima Torii, one of the "Three Beautiful Scenes" of Japan

Osaka Castle

Yoyogi National Gymnasium,
Kenzo Tange architect, Tokyo
———
Portopia Hotel, Kobe

ALONE AND IN GROUPS:
THE ONE AND THE MANY

Woman in kimono and bullet train,
Atami Station

Schoolgirls in Roppongi, Tokyo

At the fish market, *kamasu* display, on Tokyo Bay

Monk playing recorder, Ueno Park, Tokyo

FACES OF WAR: NATIVES AND GAIJIN

Statue of Lord Date, Sendai

War Memorial, Hiroshima

Monument of Commodore Perry, Kurihama, on Tokyo Bay

Glover Garden, Nagasaki Bay (setting for *Mme Butterfly*)

FUNCTION AND ELEGANCE:
THEN AND NOW

Thatched storage hut, Okinawa

Old Kyoto Alley

Po Mo architecture, Jean-Paul Gaultier Boutique, Tokyo

Capsule Building, Kisho Kurokawa architect, Tokyo

SACRED AND PROFANE:
NATURE AS ARTIFICE

Statue of Basho at Umibe Bridge, Fukagawa, Tokyo

Rice Field, Chiba

Mannequins on the sidewalk, Ginza, Tokyo

———

Po Mo Ikibana [flower arrangement], Kyoto Gosho

KIYOMI AND KUMIKO MIKUNI

Why? Why are men such grumps about foreign foods? I mean Japanese men, of course. Is it the taste of their mother's cooking that they desperately miss? Their wives adapt, glide easily into Western cuisines.

Well, I am not Japanese, and my mother never cooked, but after a week in Japan I experience light withdrawal symptoms. Any familiar food will do: pizza, pasta, a hamburger, kebab, and, if I can afford it—the prices may put you in debtor's prison—French haute cuisine.

That's where Mikuni comes in. Oh, there are some great French restaurants in Tokyo, all nudging Michelin's three stars out of heaven: Pastorale at the Seiyo Hotel, Maestro in Ark Hills, Apicius and L'Osier in the Ginza. But Kiyomi Mikuni, and his lovely, willowy wife, Kumiko, give the Hôtel de Mikuni its particular succulence and grace.

Of course, as in so much else in Tokyo, the name is a free-spirited misnomer. The place is no hotel at all. It is the sliver of a town house, with a diminutive front garden, next to a tiny chapel, on a secret back street—no taxi driver can ever find it—yet only a home run away from the Akasaka Palace, where former President Bush recovered from his—no, no, it's bad taste to speak of it here.

Mikuni? He hails from the village of Mashike in Hokkaido, the scion of fishermen. His father taught him to cook fish minutes out of the sea. After junior high school, he worked in a rice shop, then as a *com-*

mis in the Sapporo Grand Hotel. Taught himself French and how to make a *croque monsieur*. Learned enough to make his way to Tokyo, to wash dishes in the Imperial Hotel, under the watchful eye of Chef Nobuo Murakami.

The story is part of a colossal success story, that of postwar Japan itself. Still, you wonder: how does a fisherman's son make it, at the age of twenty, to the kitchen of the Japanese ambassador in Geneva, the kitchen—better still, the soccer team—of Fredy Girardet in Crissier, the best kitchens of France, and thence to Tokyo's culinary peak? "J'ai une bouche," I have a mouth, he says to me with a broad smile that spreads his raffish, black beard over his face. But Kumiko won't quite let it go at that. A hint of a frown puckers her smooth brow as she says: "Hataraki bachi, he works like a bee. He works even in his sleep." Then with a demure smile: "Do you know, there's only one Tokyo restaurant listed in *Relais et Châteaux?*" The smile becomes more demure as she points to her nose.

Kiyomi speaks to me in French, addressing me familiarly as *tu;* Kumiko speaks in English. When Sally and I go upstairs after dinner to the luxurious, closet-size bar, we speak as a foursome in two languages, with a smattering of Japanese to ease things along—that always pleases the Japanese. We speak of other chefs discreetly, very discreetly; we speak of France, and how Japan has changed.

Japan, at least Tokyo, has become ultrasophisticated since I first visited in the mid-seventies, since Kiyomi worked as a *commis*. Kumiko sits across from us, clad in pearls and a claret Givenchy; Kiyomi, without his toque, is in spotless whites. He remains open, *sans façon;* a rascal light rises easily to his eyes. His best friend is a pug-nosed former boxer who runs A Ta Gueule (literally, "in your mug") in Ebisu. It is a small, inexpensive Franco-Japanese bistro, with some of the freshest fish in town—and that's saying a great deal.

On a Sunday night, the Mikunis invite us to A Ta Gueule. We arrive before they do, and the little bantam chef, Tanabe, does not bow to us from his kitchen counter—he winks. The Mikunis punctually appear, in Ralph Lauren his-and-hers cashmere sweaters. Mussels in white wine, Vouvray, char-grilled bass with fennel, tarte Tatin. Kiyomi wryly deprecates some prizes he has won in France. A pause, repletion. Then he shakes his head: "Mais le Japon, le Japon, s'a changé." Kiyomi cannot forget the Sea of Japan brine in his veins. Kumiko, a Tokyo girl, puts a dainty dollop of whipped cream in her espresso and says nothing. She knows there's no going back. As we leave, Tanabe comes to the door, his eyes black slits of merriment. He presents Sally with a large shopping bag: inside is an enormous raw cabbage, as fine as any bouquet of roses.

At one time in his career, Kiyomi Mikuni had learned the aesthetic of dazzling ice sculpture from a grand master of that culinary art, Shuhou Okutomi. But ice, in the end, must melt. I think of Japan now, of people like Suki, like Kiyomi and Kumiko, and wonder what will remain when the dazzle fades, the artifice melts. Will it still be that irreducible element we call old Japan?

INTERNATIONALISM OR CHANGE?

Yoshi and Isono, two of my graduate students, are members of a friendly, youthful, Japanese army, thirty-seven thousand strong, which annually invades American campuses. They study eagerly, study everything. Does this mean that Japan is "internationalizing," as the shibboleth goes? As an Egyptian-born American, the question strikes me as mildly absurd. How can any nation—certainly not America, certainly not Egypt—maintain a dream of purity and permanence, as if it were the very shadow of eternity?

From its beginnings in the mists of prehistory, from the neolithic cultures of Jomon (rope-patterned pottery), Japan has of course continually changed. It changed critically in the early centuries of our era, through the Nara and Heian Periods (710–794, 794–1192), during which it absorbed, from China and Korea, Confucianism and Buddhism, absorbed culture, script, law. Japan changed with every shift in the winds of war through feudal times, the Kamakura (1192–1333) and Muromachi (1333–1603) Periods, until Tokugawa Ieyasu and his descendants held the country in their fossil grip for nearly two and a half centuries. The Meiji Restoration (1868) marked the start of modern Japan, opening itself across Asia to Europe and across the Pacific to America.

A Portuguese ship stranded on the southern island of Tane-gashima in 1543, followed six years later by Saint Francis Xavier and his implacable missionaries, gave the Japanese a taste of things foreign for nearly a century. But by 1639, the Tokugawa shogunate had had enough. Japan declared a state of *sakoku* and slammed the door shut on the world—except for a peephole, the tiny island of Dejima, off Nagasaki, through which only some Dutch and Chinese licensed merchants could trade. (Ironically, the earlier introduction of Western matchlock guns may have contributed to the unification of Japan, starting with Oda Nobu-naga in 1573.)

In the histories of internationalization, though, the inescapable reference is Commodore Matthew Perry, whose Black Ships fate-fully appeared off Uraga, near Edo (later Tokyo) Bay, in 1853. (Perry's portentous monument, streaked with dark, weathered stripes, still stands in a bleak park at nearby Kurihama, adjoining the industrial waterfront; Japanese schoolchildren visit it; Ameri-cans waiting for the ferry to cross Tokyo Bay ignore it.) When Perry returned the following year, Japan was ready for him, not with guns but treaties—treaties because no kamikaze (divine wind) came to destroy the ominous ships, as it had once dis-persed the invading fleet of the Mongol hordes. The commodore proved farsighted as well as magnanimous: "Many years will not elapse," he wrote, "before this magnificent country will be num-bered among the most important of the eastern nations." Japan opened reluctantly, and that reluctance has never disappeared. Yet the country's annual, trillion-dollar transactions with the world betray an interdebtedness hard to ignore or conceal.

Shuichi Kato put it this way: "When the Black Ships appeared off Japan's shores, Japan was entirely devoid of a system of ab-solute values based on belief in an absolute being. . . . Such a state of affairs was undoubtedly highly favorable to the introduction of foreign ideas." At the same time, this same lack of transcendent values—other than loyalty to the group—inhibited the creation of utopian or radical ideas that effect "fundamental social transformations." Thus, paradoxically, indeed miraculously, Japan *seems* to borrow endlessly without change, maintaining dual styles within a single identity. Or as the slogan goes: "Japanese spirit, Western learning."

Forget for the moment the frenzied borrowings, the alternations between xenomania and xenophobia, in fact their coexistence, during the Meiji Period. Forget also the resentment some Japanese still feel when one of them succeeds signally abroad and the awe they still feel for that same foreign success. Consider, instead, the crisscrossing currents of our own epoch.

America's influence on Japan is obvious; the reverse influence, though less obvious, is ever more palpable. Yet influence is not really the word to describe relations between major centers of economic and cultural power. These relations may include translation, adaptation, appropriation, assimilation, cooptation—and also plain rejection. Hence, instead of influence, I say transaction. For the model is always changed in cultural replication; something is lost and something gained; and the idea of an "original," in a time of simulacra, carries no conviction. I paraphrase the poet James Merrill: All life is translation, and we are all lost in it.

One curious instance of "translation" may suffice. Louis Alvarez went to make a documentary in Japan, "The Japanese Version," about appropriations of American culture. He saw Japanese businessmen all dressed up as cowboys, riding horses and roping steer. It was a scene from central casting. When he remarked to their leader, a man called Doc Suzuki, that the American cowboy represented the quintessential loner, Doc replied: "You're wrong. For us, the cowboy myth is all about working together. . . . Cowboys got together around the campfire to solve problems. It's all about teamwork." Whether cowboys or baseball players, whatever Japan may import, it still adheres to its own cultural interpretation.

Japan, we know, exports, sometimes dumps its products on foreign markets. But while Japanese products invade America, the English language invades the Japanese (see later, under Japlish). American businessmen learn Bushido, American prairie towns feature sushi bars, and countless American yuppies romance their Acuras or sip Napa Valley Chardonnay owned by Suntory Distilleries. Some have even learned to say *arigato gozaimasu* (thank you) and *ohayo gozaimasu* (good morning).

I do not mean that differences between Japan and America are vanishing. How can they, when the Japanese serve a glass of water two-thirds full and the Americans serve it brimming with ice? I mean, rather, that the whole question of "internationalization," of cultural difference—when it should be preserved, when overcome, when both preserved and overcome—has become rife in our world, as has the question of cultural identity. It is not only that the Japanese find it difficult to perceive Americans, Americans the Japanese; it is also that the Japanese find it difficult to perceive themselves, the Americans to perceive themselves. (In this regard, the Japanese prove more tolerant of ambiguities, the Americans of differences.) The solution to these intricacies of alterity is often unexpected—that is to say, the solution may take an imaginative rather than an ideological turn.

In the great film of Alain Resnais and Marguerite Duras, Hiroshima, Mon Amour, for instance, the difference between the two lovers seems invincible. The film starts with the couple naked, embracing in bed. The Japanese man calmly, flatly, says, in French, "You saw nothing in Hiroshima. Nothing." The French woman, calmly, flatly, says, "I saw everything. Everything." Apparently, these two orders of experience are incommensurable. Nudity, language, even love cannot overcome the difference. Or can they? The handsome actor, Eiji Okada, who plays the man, has vaguely Western features, as Emmanuelle Riva, who plays the woman, has a touch of Asia around the eyes. This cannot be accidental. About the man, Duras says:

> A Japanese actor with pronounced Japanese features might lead people to believe that it is especially because the protagonist is Japanese that the French actress was attracted to him. Thus, whether we liked it or not, we'd find ourselves caught again in the trap of "exoticism," and the involuntary racism inherent in any exoticism.
>
> The spectator should not say "How attractive Japanese men are," but "How attractive *that man* is."
>
> This is why it is preferable to minimize the difference between the two protagonists. If the audience never forgets that this is the story of a Japanese man and a French woman, the profound implications of the film are lost. If the audience does forget it, these profound implications become apparent.

Here, then, is an imaginative solution, a human solution as well, to a particular case of difference or alterity. Here is internationalization at work, as it should work, though tragic in this film's case. And the solution suggests at once the concrete and the universal, something partaking of both, a transaction across languages, cultures, genders, even wars, a translation without original, a mutuality sustained by need, sympathy, eroticism—sustained at its limit by love—all rendered in Duras's magnificent art.

Indeed, art sustains our interactive world no less than commerce or travel. Again, Shuichi Kato makes the main point in his *Form, Style, Tradition: Reflections on Japanese Art and Society:*

> When one looks at this general configuration from a Japanese vantage point, it is apparent that it was not only Japan that was "opened up" following the end of World War II. In the mid-nineteenth century, when Japan first set about the commercial and technological opening-up of the nation, the art and literature of the West were still closed. Today, in the mid-twentieth century, when Japan has embarked on an intellectual opening-up of the nation, the art and literature of the West are also far more open. There is no reason to suppose that the indigestion induced in Japan before World War II by the one-sided introduction of Western culture will occur again as a result of the exchanges of this postwar era. Both sides have changed too much for that. The importance of the other side's having changed lies in its bearing on the universality of the concept of art. Once a universal concept is created, no matter who is responsible, it belongs to everybody. We have already accepted that idea where science is concerned, and almost certainly, in the years ahead, we shall come to accept it in contemporary art as well.

Art may be "universal" in different cultures in slightly different ways. Still, contemporary art has accepted the idea of universality with parodic vengeance. The artist Yasumasa Morimura, for instance, repaints, with the help of photomontage and computer imaging, the masterpieces of European art, substituting his own face for every face, male or female, in the original. Thus, Rembrandt's *Anatomy Lesson,* Velasquez's *Las Meninas,* Manet's *Olympe,* van Gogh's *Self-Portrait with Pipe and Bandaged Ear,* all stare back at us with Asiatic eyes. They stare not only across the ages, but also across cultural values, identities, meanings, in a virtuoso exercise of artistic no less than anthropological irony. One wonders: can anything be at once more particular and also more universal than these purloined images?

Not all change, however, depends on cunning appropriations. Change has come to Japan from within, even if the distinction between outside and inside in the end serves only suspicious minds.

Consider women (see also later, under Marriage). Despite Article 14 of the Japanese Constitution guaranteeing women equal status under the law, that equality has been a widely shared social fiction. The fiction, though, may be slowly, ever so slowly, turning into fact. In 1992, a judge awarded a compensation of $12,400 to a woman for *seku hara* (sexual harassment) in the workplace. The ruling has no precedent in all Japanese history. Are women effecting a Velvet Revolution? Is their role as infinitely self-abnegating mothers changing? As always in Japan, women control the purse strings at home; now they spend the purse abroad. In twos or twenties, they go on tours; they entertain themselves generously in the best Ginza restaurants; they streak around Tokyo in racy sports cars. This does not mean they can also race up various career ladders. But their growing social presence, like their crescive purchasing or political power, has become irrevocable. And their urge for independence, for a room of their own, receives recognition in serious films like Takehiro Nakajima's *Okoge* about a woman and two gay men who all refuse to conform.

Or consider lifestyles. The Japanese consume less rice, more bread, meat, and dairy products, more junk food of every kind, than they did a few decades ago. They retire later, but work shorter hours, down from the recent 2,152 hours a year, closer to the American norm of 1,898 hours. They save a little less, consume much more. Still, the Japanese, whose longevity is highest in the world, continue to save, providing, like good Confucians—the Master survives more securely in Japan than in China—not only for children but for grandchildren as well. Thus, continuity grapples across the generations with change, and even older leaders call on their people to alter their ways.

Mr. Sony, for instance—I mean, of course, the visionary Akio Morita—now calls for a kinder, gentler Japan, so to speak, calls specifically for a "new management philosophy" suitable for a more open society in which, as personal expectations rise, many begin to mutter about the "cost of growth," "the quality of life." And Yoshio Hatano, Japan's ambassador to the United Nations—a man of genuine and practical idealism—thinks it is time for Japan to cease boasting about its "ethnic purity," time for it to assume its global responsibilities and become a "leisure as well as an economic superpower."

In two decades, I have seen Japan metamorphose, and I have seen it remain the same. I have seen the black Japanese limousines—the Nissan Presidents, the Toyota Centurys—yield to Mercedes 500s and BMW 700s. (Only the *yakuza*, the gangsters, continue to buy hulking Cadillacs because of their "bulletproof" construction.) I have seen Tokyo restaurants like Maestro, Mikuni, and Maxim's fill with smart, bejewelled women in Western designer clothes, and the mammoth Metropolitan City Hall rise above the fumes of the capital. I have seen "mansions" (apartment houses, really) go up in every style from Japanese Tudor to Postmodern Kitsch. I have seen "indoor ski resorts" take their place next to urban, steel-meshed, high-rise golf driving ranges. I have seen, in remote little seaports like Otaru in Hokkaido, *Les Musts de Cartier* nestle between local pottery shops. I have seen the giant, plaster hands of the Mona Lisa resting delicately on the marquee of a *pachinko* parlor in Shibuya, and seen on television a samurai film—desperate duels, ambushes, insurrections, flaming human torches—play to a background of hard rock. (Where's the contradiction anyway?) I have seen Japanese men step back and hold open the door for their spouses, and Japanese waiters pour wine to women before men. And I have seen, withal, the shadow of resentment fall on impassive Japanese faces as they watched the *narikin*, or even more disparagingly, the *baburu yaro* (bubble guys) glitter by. Most shockingly perhaps, I have seen AIDS discussed as a disease from which Japan is not somehow exempt—not after those organized sex tours to Thailand. In brief, change may have widened the gap between generations in Japan more than in America.

What, then, has remained the same? Small answers come to mind: rice paddies with white herons at the edge; outhouses; crisp ten thousand–yen bills; *mochi* cakes for the new year; origami displays in temples, schools, stores; cherry blossom viewing in the spring; first graders in uniforms, a tremolo of yellow or red or blue caps; corner sushi bars, *soba* shops, yakitori tents, offering late night snacks; male graduates of Todai, ruling the bureaucratic roosts; huge, paper, carp streamers flying over glistening tile roofs, announcing the number of male children in the house, on *kodomo no hi* (Boy's Day); *omamori*, protective talismans, everywhere; peddlers in the streets chanting through loudspeakers, "Yaki imo" (roasted yams) or "Takeya saodake" (laundry poles); imperishable bamboo groves; a thousand other things.

After all, several millennia of Japanese history cannot dissolve without leaving a trace in the Japanese psyche. The trace was still deep at the end of the Meiji Period, when Lafcadio Hearn wrote in *Kokoro*, "All that Japan has been able to do so miraculously well has been done without any [emotional] self-transformation." Nearly a century later, Ian Buruma, long a resident of Japan, remarked in *Behind the Mask*, "Although Japan today on the surface seems more advanced and modern than, say, decaying Britain, underneath she is in many ways closer to the European Middle Ages, before Christianity obliterated the last vestiges of paganism."

In the end, we will only know how much Japan has changed or remained the same when the young today, who pretend to be so different from their elders, have become themselves middle-aged. Then may we determine what, if anything, has really altered in Japanese society, in the Japanese character. For tourists and even expatriates cannot discern the full measure of that inner change.

LADY IN A LARGE HAT
An Imaginary Portrait

That's how I see her, in a large, stunningly fashionable hat, half hiding her face. She is a Japanese expatriate, living in London, or Rome, or Paris. Let us say Paris. After all, what chic woman could resist becoming *parisienne?*

But why expatriation? It is rare enough in Japan. "Oh, modern Japanese culture is a little thin, a little insecure," she whispers vaguely. But her gimlet eyes—no, I see them as glittering serpent's eyes—belie her vagueness. The lady detests insecurity.

Besides, Paris suits her. People are *sec,* brittle, dry. And if they are not always intelligent, they are impatient, unsmiling, even rude enough to be mistaken for smart. She has had her fill of the bowing and smiling. She knows what she wants.

She has wanted out. All those *histoires de famille* in Japan, all the vicious wrangling. True, she was a *fille à papa.* So what? She wants now to recreate her world, sculpt it with a scalpel out of flesh, tendons, erogenous zones, bones. Her will, like her father's, was always preternaturally, prenatally, fierce.

Will, wealth, smarts—yes, even street smarts—realism in the marrow, a sense of discrimination (or is it snobbery?) bred into the bone, how could the lady fail to make Paris her home? How better to avenge unspeakable miseries that may still gnaw on the brain?

And the amorous adventures. Here France and Japan hold hands and turn up their noses at puritans. The lady likes the French: they can be handsome, they disdain sentimental dross. I imagine her with hunky young painters affecting ponytails, sullen young writers, their fingertips yellow with nicotine. They are all difficult enough to challenge her dominion. But dominate she will, then move on. *Passez outre,* Gide's Theseus used to say. At first predatory, her sexuality sublimates itself with the passing years into status, show. Either way, no holds barred, no quarter given or received. Madame Butterfly strikes mercilessly back.

But does she really like the French? In a tight knot of her psyche, does she not still believe in Japanese superiority/inferiority? That belief requires a certain innocence. After three decades in Paris, you learn a little irony, a little cynicism—you learn the uses of bad faith. The latter is not so very different, after all, from Japanese "face." You muffle conscience, muffle dreary self-criticism; you put on the best face. In the process, cultural chauvinism becomes raw egotism. In this universal trait, pretensions of Japanese uniqueness dissolve.

I can see the lady's eyes narrow beneath the hat—she wore it once before at Longchamp, or was it Auteuil? Then she laughs scornfully, and a crystal champagne glass shatters in my hand. *Mon ami,* she seems to say, I am beyond all that nationalist prattle. Her fastidiousness hardens as she moves watchfully in the beau monde. Nowadays, she insists on a curriculum vitae before meeting strangers.

The Lady in the Large Hat: does she represent the future of Japan, its past, or something atemporal and eternally present? I am certain she keeps by her bed a brocaded copy of Sei Shonagon's acerbic masterpiece, *The Pillow Book.* I am certain, too, she has no habitation more particular than mind or malice or a desert saint has.

But then, this is only the certainty of fantasy. I wish I could meet the lady who tramps through such conceits. Or do I?

PART IV
EDUCATION

HIROKO WASHIZU

She has a round face and round eyes and so looks either perpetually jovial or perpetually bemused. A shade plump for a Japanese, she still moves swiftly, her smart business suits giving her allure. She can outdrink, outthink most men and lives alone. Once she was married, but following her honeymoon, she resolved to study Nathaniel Hawthorne in America. Her headstrong ways—what had she learned from Hester?—did not make for a Japanese marriage made in heaven. The divorce came within two years. Now, in early middle age, she has a doctorate—rare among Japanese scholars, male or female—in American literature.

I think of Hiroko as brave, headlong, a little wacky with charm, a woman caught by social change in Japan but riding high on the wave.

A little wacky but lucid. Sally asked her one day, "Hiroko, do you really belong in Japan?" She answered, "I belong nowhere else." Then after a pause: "Because I am neither mother nor wife, I cannot belong in Japan either." But she shows no grudge. She drinks and jokes with men, can become as mindless as they are after the fifth thimble of sake, and knows Shinjuku's bars like the back of her hand. Sober, she is as reliable as any of them on the job, but never as charmless. She teaches at Seijo University, Rikkyo University, other universities. (Like many other Japanese professors, she routinely teaches at several institutions to make ends meet.)

In her cups, Hiroko may become boisterous, never bitter. "Mind your business," she may snap, if asked jokingly about her lovers. But the rebuke vanishes when she laughs, white teeth glistening; her round cheeks press upward against eyes become thin merry lines. I do wonder, though, how long the merriness lasts when Hiroko returns to her tiny flat. Like most Japanese academics, perhaps like most academics everywhere, the life of the mind does not fill her life to the brim.

I think of Hiroko as a triumphant victim of Japan, though—how un-American—she does not think of herself that way. Few men there would marry a divorcée, fewer a woman with an advanced degree, fewer still one so willful and bright. Still, where else would a woman alone find so much loyalty among friends—or simple safety on the streets? Where would an eccentric, so long as she plays by a few immutable rules in the workplace, encounter such wide and tacit acceptance? Knowing this, Hiroko will not leave Japan or become, like some Japanese émigrés, deformed.

When I see Hiroko Washizu scamper down a corridor between classrooms, propelled by a zest of ineffable origin, I think she hurries full of, no, not just energy, equivocal grace. And I think how much Japan continues to waste its women.

THE QUEST FOR
TRANSCULTURAL VALUES

Every society makes its great truce with time. The truce has many names. One of the names is education, which both resists and accedes to change. But the question has now become how educate on a planet so fractious yet inexorably interactive, where cultures collide every nanosecond and signs lose themselves in newer signs?

The most common answer, this side of platitude, is that education in the postmodern world must be at once local and global, a search for transcultural values. It must be so because knowledge itself both specifies and generalizes, and the world we all inhabit has become a hybrid, heterogeneous, hodgepodge field of concerns. This does not make the earth a safer place, as Salman Rushdie tragically knows—his very life has been caught between the old "apostles of purity" and the new "apostles of mongrelization," as has the life of his translator, knifed to death by a fanatic at Tsukuba University.

These geopolitical facts may jar insular Japan more than immigrant America. For the latter has learned to translate cultures—"cross the border, close the gap," Leslie Fiedler prophetically cried—translate even when it stammers violently. The translations include experiments in multicultural education.

Such words, though, hint piety; reality is more intractable and ludicrous. There is a joke. An American businessman goes to Japan to lecture on managerial practices. He can't speak Japanese, of course, and so he enlists the services of an experienced Japanese interpreter. As the American commences to speak, the interpreter says to the Japanese audience through their earphones: "American speaker is beginning with what Americans call 'Joke.' We do not know why Americans do this, but we must be polite. At the end of 'Joke,' we must laugh and applaud. I will tell you when." The American by now is well into his story, and the interpreter alerts his audience: "It's coming soon now." The American finishes his story, the interpreter gives his signal, the audience bursts out laughing and applauds. Beaming, the American says to the audience, "I've told this joke many times, but you people are the first to appreciate it really. Thank you."

So much for translation, cultural or linguistic, in which we are indeed all lost. Even humor can not wholly transcend its circumstances. How can education, then, do so? When I see Japanese boys and girls, just out of school in their dark blue uniforms—always segregated—see them, lumpy or lanky, move with newly acquired decorum, callow restraint, I think of my own school days. Here is what I wrote in a slim memoir called Out of Egypt:

I experienced much grief when I began to attend government schools. These proved intellectually demanding, socially bruising, physically dismal, proved altogether traumatic for me. At the grilled, lead-hued gate of the school, which shut at five minutes past eight with frightening finality and opened mercifully again at five minutes to four, the parental Rolls or Daimler might wait for the most privileged pupils. But once inside, these abandoned all hope. Jostling with the rest, they relied on their wits, fists, and unbreakable skulls—a quick, sharp blow with the head to the enemy's nosebridge—to absolve themselves daily of cowardice, effeminacy, or simply good breeding. In the brief recreation periods, the younger boys played *el beel* (marbles), viciously throwing their nickel leaders at a triangle full of bright, multicolored spheres. Older boys played *fudbol* (soccer) with a makeshift lump of old socks, delighting to kick each other in the shins. Lunch was a predatory affair, wolves and hyenas, the stronger or hungrier fighting for inedible gobs of glutinous matter while *el alpha* (the monitor), disdained by all, tried to establish some order of precedence around the table. (For many, poorer pupils, this was their only meal of the day.) Extracurricular activities? Suspect. Character development? Absurd. The fit survived, and everyone studied grimly or else fell by the way.

How far have I really moved beyond those dread days? I like to think that, crossing the Atlantic, I have come part of the way, though part of me may remain lost in *translatio*, in the passage or translation. And what have I found in American education to make up for the loss? Something akin to the power of self-creation? Would I have found that power in a Japanese university? Hardly. Education is always embedded in societies, their needs, traditions, beliefs, prejudices, embedded even in their violence.

Let me recall, then, briefly if I must, some features of American society, before attending to *paideia*, educational practices.

AMERICAN VOICES

I can speak of America only in three—at least, three—voices. One voice is cranky, sometimes strident. It rasps: "America a Puritan country? Give me a break! Call it, rather, a riot of self-indulgence. Others say: slack, sloppy, slovenly, slapdash. Well, perhaps. But we don't need Japanese politicians, looking for votes and diversions from their own scandals, to recite our lacks. In any case, American workers are not lazy; they labor longer hours (164 more hours a year) than they did two decades ago, far longer than their German counterparts. Ah, but it's quality, not the clock, that counts, quality and commitment. Americans labor in a soft environment. In this, they are no different from their greedy, blustering bosses, with their gross salaries, purblind policies, and ceaseless complaints. Yes, Americans have become a whining people, a plaintiff nation, on tennis courts, in law courts, in classrooms or boardrooms. They have created a climate of instant gratification, a therapeutic society, forever in quest of the best orgasm, smartest body weight, lowest cholesterol count, loveliest facial tuck, thinnest pizza crust. They spend two billion dollars a year on dial-a-porn. What loneliness! Self-esteem is now their highest commodity, packaged in a rhetoric of self-hype. What else can you expect? America confuses desires with needs, rights with responsibilities, expectations with merits, a society superficial in depth. It trails, as Fitzgerald said, 'the foul dust of dreams.' Have these dreams bred a race of monsters—cannibals, child molesters, serial killers, predominantly male and white—in whom every fantasy becomes its own enactment? Why are fifteen thousand Americans—that's a Roman legion—shot to death every year? Is everything in this lethal Disneyland permitted? Or has America simply become a country of sleepwalkers, drifting from quick to quicker fix, courtesy of Doctor Feelgood?"

No doubt, that voice rails too stridently, too virulently. A more judicious voice might have a different timbre. For instance: "Yes, America is unwell, and education is complicit in the nation's disease. Fingers point everywhere, a thicket of fingers. They

point to Reaganism, narcissism, racism, sexism, multiculturalism, crime, poverty, illiteracy, innumeracy, drugs, gays, pollution,
television, AIDS, deficit spending, the end of the cold war,
progressive education, lagging technologies, illegal immigrants,
credit cards, the breakup of the family, the death of God, the
destruction of the literary canon, the laxity of liberals, the in-
tolerance of conservatives, the ozone hole. Worse—or better, de-
pending upon your point of view—polls find that 53 percent
of Americans no longer care if their country leads the world.
Whatever the finger, wherever it points, the index shows change.
Values, styles, power structures shift. Meanwhile, laws substitute
for civic virtues; bureaucracy supplants morality. But society, as
William James knew, is a fabric of trust. 'Our faith,' he wrote,
'is faith in someone else's faith, and in the greatest matters this
is most the case.' That faith has frayed, and educators have done
little to renew the fabric of trust. The acrimonious debates about
multiculturalism, political correctness, and the canon of literacy
are not academic; they express profound social anxieties. Their
acrimony, their remorseless partisanship, their lack of intellectual
scruple and common civility—so much learning, so much intelligence, in the service of tendentiousness—also betray the growing alienation of the university from mainstream values. Perhaps
America has suffered too long from disrepair in its human and
physical infrastructures; perhaps, with the end of the cold war
and the resurgence of nations defeated in the last war, America
has become bemused, even bruised, in its identity."

A third voice breaks in here, rambunctious, unabashedly triumphalist: "Nonsense. This funk is unseemly in the world's sole
superpower. In 1991 only, America won the 'mother of all battles' with a few hundred casualties and won a millennial struggle with communism. Where is Khruschev now, who banged the

table with an ugly shoe and vowed to bury us? Since 1910, the United States has remained, as all the statistics prove, the richest and most productive economy in the world. The purchasing power of its average citizen is 17 percent greater than a German's, 22 percent greater than that of a Japanese. True, Japan is catching up fast. But as the former vice president of the ruling Liberal Democratic Party put it, 'Japan can exist because the United States exists, but it is not the other way around. We owe our prosperity to the United States. Many Japanese forget this fact.' Perhaps Shin Kanemaru was being politic, perhaps he was being truthful; the matter is finally in our, not another's hands.

"And what about our universities? Twenty, perhaps thirty, of them are indisputably preeminent in the world. Students around the earth flock to them in ever larger numbers, at their own cost. Why should they not? Where are classrooms more open? Where do university presses publish more books? Where do libraries have more to offer scholars or students? Indeed, where is knowledge more consistently generated and preserved? American Nobelists, nearly two hundred now, number nearly thrice the British, next in line. And what about the stanchless flood of immigrants, European, Asian, Latino, who often risk their lives to start a new life in America? However tarnished the Statue of Liberty may seem to disaffected Americans, it can still raise its torch in Beijing or Prague, Tijuana or Dhaka. America may be entitled to a bit of wallow in a recession, but it should also recall its immense recuperative powers. The 'American Century' is about to end—what other nation can better seize the twenty-first century?"

None of these voices, of course, can convey the whole truth, though together they may hint at where the truth hides. In any case, I wanted simply to emphasize that educational issues are also social, indeed geopolitical, issues.

EDUCATION: JAPAN

But what, now, of education in Japan? I hazard some generalizations. The first is that education in Japan seems nearly a mirror image of American education. Leona Esaki, president of Tsukuba University and a Nobelist in physics, puts it more precisely: "Japan educates the most talented youths in areas that produce national wealth, such as engineering. In contrast, youths in the United States favor fields that usually produce individual wealth, such as law and medicine." The second generalization is that Japanese education, especially precollege education, is highly centralized, purposeful, and conservative; that is, knowledge serves mainly to socialize, indeed to Japanize, the young. In this regard, the Mombusho (Ministry of Education) has proven wondrously and continuously effective; though it may issue every five or ten years "An Outline of Revision of the Course of Study in Japan," nothing essential alters. The results are there for all to see: Japan heads the class of nations in literacy, numeracy, realized pedagogical goals.

Unfortunately, that cranky, ill-bred voice within me cannot be stilled; it needs to rasp and rail again: "Call that an education, a liberal education? I call it a machine for conformity. Call it conformity or *wa* (harmony), it ends by turning knowledge into consensual myths. Yes, myths. Ask a bright high school graduate who can outscore any Western student in math—ask him what he has learned in school about the Rape of Nanjing, Pearl Harbor, the Burma Railroad, the Bridge on the River Kwai, the Bataan Death March, the one hundred thousand Korean 'comfort women,' or Japanese colonial rule in East Asia, from Manchuria to Malaysia. Ask his teachers as well. (The current fashion, as in Kurosawa's recent film, *Rhapsody in August*, is for the Japanese to pose as the *victims* of Pearl Harbor.) Sure, a few Japanese professors raise their small voices against amnesiac textbooks. But the Ministry of Education will overrule or outlive them all. Sure, those Japanese high school students know twice as much as their American counterparts. But what do you exactly mean by 'know?' To pass a test with high scores is not to know. Besides, they have jukus here, schools to prepare you for exams, exams to prepare you for schools, and schools to prepare you for other schools—all costing money and so more available to the rich than the poor. It's an iron escalator, which even Prime Minister Miyazawa can't stop, going from the right maternity ward (hence kindergarten), through 'proper' schools, straight up to Todai Law School Heaven. Think I'm kidding about heaven? Well, there's a story. A Japanese woman of good family suddenly asks her gaijin boyfriend to stop seeing her for a while. Her sister has become engaged to a Todai graduate, she explains, and her whole family is undergoing a check. They've all decided to be careful under these very special circumstances. Rikai shite (please understand). Or did I misunderstand the story? Anyway, to come down from heaven: I can't speak much Japanese, so I won't speak about the aptitude of Japanese students in foreign languages. All I know is that six years of school English comes to zilch. Well, maybe not zilch—those youngsters like to say 'Haro' on the street. That much they can say without feeling they have lost their Japanese identity in foreign babble or surrendered to the language of the victors. As to university education in the humanities, it's just a four-year holiday. True, those college kids are neat and ever so polite. They bow when they come to class at all, come half an hour late, and chat quietly with friends in the back rows—they come to class mainly to visit a little with one another. The serious students, four or five, sit right up front. They have been elected by the rest to take careful notes, which they copy for friends so that all can pass the exam. Well, those serious students could have spared themselves the trouble: hardly anybody flunks. And why begrudge them the time of their lives? They worked so hard to get in, and after graduation, they'll work even harder till they die or retire. Besides, why pick on the students? Do you think their professors are much better? They rarely comment on student papers, cancel classes, arrive late, sometimes switch from a prestigious university to a more relaxed institution—the work is easier, the pay the same."

Here I have to shut up that ignorant, crabby voice before it embarrasses us all. Another, more measured voice takes over.

"Every society develops the educational system it needs, perhaps deserves. Criticism, therefore, must be contextual, must come mostly from within. Still, Bakhtin was right when he wrote, 'In the realm of culture, outsideness is a most powerful factor in understanding.' As an outsider, I can try to understand Japanese education, especially higher education, by asking certain questions. For instance:

"Is college or university education too specialized, too particular? In my experience, discussions with Japanese students, and even with adults, can become quickly thin, not only because of their shyness, limited English, and reluctance to disagree, but also because they lack intellectual scope. Americans may have gone too far in diffusing the curriculum, the Japanese in focusing it. This is not wholly accidental: for the Japanese, specialization implies loyalty, purity. Thus a few canonical authors—Poe, Hawthorne, Melville, James, Faulkner—get all the attention in American literature. But extreme particularism in the university ends by acting conservatively, for it precludes any general principle of change.

"Another question comes to mind: how pervasively authoritarian is the Japanese university, and what impact does such an attitude have on both creativity and criticism? The authoritarianism of the classroom reflects, of course, a larger tendency in Japanese society; the Mombusho, an academic colleague put it to me, orders professors to appear for hearings. True, in Japan there is consensus in hierarchy, in authority consensus. But knowledge also thrives on debate, dispute, criticism; and innovation, in art or science, requires independence, resistance, rejection. In Japan, however, both knowledge and creation serve a loftier goal: harmony, duration of the group. This has led Kurt Singer to say, 'It is one of the most characteristic traits of Japanese life that it has reduced the realm of [individual] genius to a bare minimum, with a rigour unknown in any other great civilization.'

"There is also the question of self-transformation, self-knowledge. Can we ask how much of Japanese higher education encourages introspection, self-examination, confrontation with the self? Many observers have remarked the lack of inner struggle, lack of irony, dialectic, contradiction, in many Japanese students. They appear naive, innocent, almost bland, not only because they have learned impassiveness—none of those distracting Western tics and gestures—but perhaps because, lacking interiority, they are in harmony with their environment; they belong wholly to their culture. Conflicts in them are not fought out but either avoided or resolved in intricate ritual forms. The question remains: how can the Japanese act, without inner direction, in an alien environment? What can education contribute to thought and behavior in a global context, in an intermingling world, where native proprieties no longer serve?"

A third voice breaks in here with disciplined impatience: "Please! You'll remind us next how abominably some Japanese behave when they go abroad. Well, so do Americans, despite their vaunted individualism. Yes, indeed, education coextends with a particular culture, a specific environment. The questions you raise are, therefore, ethnocentric. Forgive me, but the questions also rely on stereotypes. Have you read Stevenson and

Stigler's *The Learning Gap*? It shows that Japanese grade schools practice what American schools only preach, that John Dewey is more alive in Tokyo than in New York. And have you read the Confucian text, *Ta Hsueh: The Great Digest*, which the Japanese honor? It says, 'The men of old wanting to clarify and diffuse throughout the empire that light which comes from looking strait into the heart and then acting . . . sought precise verbal definitions of their inarticulate thoughts.' Is that not self-knowledge? We honor teachers in Japan. Do you? Our school year is nearly two months longer than yours. Why is that? And our bills carry portraits of our writers and educators: Natsume Soseki (¥1,000), professor at Tokyo University; Inazo Nitobe (¥5,000), educator at Hokkaido University; and Yukichi Fukuzawa (¥10,000), founder of Keio University.

"Japan is changing; a different generation is now coming into power. A generation still younger has traveled much abroad—ten million Japanese now travel every year—and may further speed the change. Yes, yes, I know, many of the travelers are repeaters. Still, no nation that trades so globally can remain forever isolated or intellectually provincial. Give Japan another decade, at most two. You'll see transformations, even in the Ministry of Education. At the same time, why drastically tamper with a formula that has brought such rapid and unparalleled success? The Japanese phoenix has risen spectacularly from its ashes. Oh, yes, Japan will change, but only in accordance with its own rhythms. If you learn this, you will understand a great deal more."

Of course, no one here is fooled: all three voices echo the same misguided gaijin. But some Japanese seem also disaffected with their own system, as Professors Iwao Nakatani and Daizaburo Hashizume show in their series of articles in the *Asahi Shimbun* (December 1991, February 1992). Have these professors suffered contamination abroad? Hardly: many other Japanese nonacademics would sustain them, for instance, Seiji Tsutsumi when he says: "The unfortunate thing about Japan is the absence of people capable of providing intellectual leadership. This is related to the existing academic system, which is designed to pass on learning rather than to stimulate creativity." The chorus is rising.

BEYOND ACADEMIC ABSTRACTIONS

What lies beyond such academic abstractions? I think about the lived experience of adolescents in Japan, how they will recollect their school days in middle age. I think how teachers support equally the brightest and dimmest in their classes, how peers rally quickly to their own—except when they bully or rag some wretched outsider to death (sometimes literally) or when they serve as punishing agents for a higher authority that a member has offended, reclaiming him only after he has earned absolution from on high. No group, for instance, would close ranks against disloyalty to the school, let alone the flag.

Perversely, I wonder, too, why so many Japanese men indulge sexual fantasies about uniformed school girls, fantasies nourished continually on film, in comic books, in assorted pornography. Are these fantasies of incest, of power and class, of nostalgia for vanished youth? I asked a Japanese friend. He smiled away his embarrassment and mumbled: "You see, at school, we were never permitted to express romantic feelings for girls. Perhaps these feelings come back when we are old." I could understand well: in Egypt, girls attended fiercely separate schools, and the image of a sloe-eyed nymph in white pinafore and knee stockings, tripping home after classes, could haunt a boy for years.

I wonder, too, about the indissoluble fraternity of college and school boys, how it uses the past to conquer the future. In Japan, the bonds of male prejudice, prestige, and shared recall form a mesh more steely than any American old boys' network. The filaments spread through universities, bureaucracies, businesses, banks; they form the very stuff of political parties, of *yakuza*, of nostalgic films—even masterpieces like Ozu's *Tokyo Story*—and of college sports.

The battles of Japan may not have been won on the playing fields of its schools, but sports create their own rituals of bonding and remembrance. Once, on a chilly, late-autumn afternoon, I saw hordes of youths, mostly boys, congregate on the pavement of a Ginza street. They all seemed privy to some immense joke. By evening, they had settled down for the night in jovial clumps, reclining on newspaper beds, improvising tables from discarded crates, snacking on homemade sushi and big bottles of beer. The next morning, the clumps had formed into an eager, silent queue, moving imperceptibly through an obscure door. I had first thought: a demonstration! Next I thought: some kind of celebration! "But what is this door now?" I asked someone in the queue. Smiles, whispers, shaken heads, fingers pointing down the line. Finally, someone who could speak three words of English said, "Tickets. Meiji-Waseda Rugby Game." I walked away, thinking, "So that's where they revisit youth, the golden years."

In Japan, experience, that of youth particularly, is heavily ritualized, mediated; it no longer seems personal experience. Because the Japanese remain, like other mortals, individuals, some feel an acute kind of loneliness, alienation, a desperation leading to suicide. Literature, film, television teem with forlorn or violent figures of youth: Japanese Werthers, hippies, dropouts, anarchists, even the gangster *nihirisuto* (nihilist), testifying each to the breakdown of collective rituals, beliefs.

For most students, though, collective experience remains both effective and affective. In this regard, the arts play a lively role. *Manga*, rock videos, and cyberpunk have not wholly displaced—

not yet, not even for the young—the artistic heritage of Japan: *waka* and haiku poetry; *The Tale of Genji* and *The Pillow Book*; ceramics, lacquer ware, calligraphy, ukiyo-e; samurai swords and *washi* fans, kimonos and gardens; No, Bunraku, or Kabuki theatre; *Nihon buyo*, *bugaku*, and *buto* dances; the *biwa*, the *koto*, the *shamisen*; *kodo* drummers. The list seems endless, endless too in disciplined beauty, tasteful ingenuity. Nor has the vital culture sustaining all these arts ceased to develop, grow. As Donald Keene remarks:

> The past survives in aesthetic preferences that often find surprising outlets for expression—a box of *sushi*, a display of lacquered *zori*, branches of artificial maple leaves along a commercial street. And the man who prides himself on his elegantly tailored Western clothes will be delighted to sit in Japanese style, destroying the creases, at a restaurant where traditional food is served with traditional elegance. The Japanese aesthetic past is not dead. It accounts for the magnificent profusion of objects of art that are produced each year.

But does this rooted, aesthetic quality of education in Japan finally enhance or inhibit empathy for other cultures, other peoples?

GLOBAL QUESTIONS

The question returns us to our initial concern: how educate in an interactive world? Confronted with the earth's boggling variety, most of us have begun to realize that, however unique we may imagine ourselves to be, we remain a case among cases. Does this lead to unqualified relativism? They do it that way, we do it this way, live and let live, we all have our separate realities. Must we, in the name of cultural tolerance, for instance, accept slavery, cannibalism, political torture, child prostitution, female circumcision, widow burning, chemical warfare, toxic pollution of the environment, grotesque historical revisionism, as local practices with which we have no business to meddle?

Or must we, in the more complex case before us, resign our-selves to permanent and mutual incomprehensions? We have our concept of fairness in trade, they have theirs. What seems to us hypocritical to them is courteous; to us naive, to them sincere; to us primitive, to them traditional; to us masochistic, to them stoical; to us cruel, to them uncompromising; to us conform-ist, to them loyal; to us mediocre, to them unostentatious.

Hardly. We do share an uncommon humanity. The mystery of other cultures becomes somehow part of our own mystery. Bon gré, mal gré, we cross boundaries, even if in crossing we lose our inner serenity, our inward ease. The choice today, then, is not between universal values (the West) and tribal harmony (Japan). The task in a shrinking world is to discover, perhaps create, new transcultural values. To this task, liberal education everywhere hopes to contribute its share—call it Einfühlung, cognitive empa-thy, or simply openness to the Other.

Still, liberal education may no more bridge the chasms of the world than learning a foreign language or dabbling for a year abroad. We need some pragmatic principles of coexistence, some tentative rules of planetary behavior, that liberal education may adumbrate but cannot enforce. Can we imagine a united nations of values, a security council of ideals rather than of entrenched interests? How can the ecology of the planet become as dear to us as a rose planted in the back yard? Where is the Archimedean point of both local and global awareness on this earth?

Here we could do worse than to invoke the American Decla-ration of Independence. "Life, liberty, and the pursuit of happi-ness" may have no metaphysical self-evidence, but they are prag-matically in high demand. V. S. Naipaul—a Trinidadian of Indian descent, educated in England, forever peregrine—called "the pursuit of happiness" a beautiful idea, easy to take for granted, easier still to misconstrue. Yet for him, born an outsider to Western civilization as I was, the idea remains "marvelous to contemplate." Naipaul breaks into rhapsody: "It is an elastic idea; it fits all men. It implies a certain kind of society, a certain kind of spirit. . . . So much is contained in it: the idea of the individual, responsibility, choice, the life of the intellect, the idea of vocation and perfectibility and achievement. It is an immense human idea. It cannot be reduced to a fixed system."

I know personally what Naipaul means. I know, too, that happiness may be construed differently in Harare and Hollywood, Cairo and Kobe. But let us not quibble unduly: happiness is found in freedom from hunger, disease, bondage, pain. I do not hesitate to offer it as a genial principle of transcultural values.

ANECDOTES OF YOUTH

Happiness, though, as we all know, demands more than freedom from pain and want; it demands dignity, self-realization, transcendence. These, I have said, express themselves variously in various cultures. There's the rub, the grating task of cultural mediation, cultural translation, a labor to which I can see no end in our time. What do the two wealthiest nations contribute to that most exigent of tasks? What, in particular, do their institutions of higher learning?

From the Japanese university, I wonder what can the world learn? From Japan itself, we can learn the virtues of rigor, cooperation, frugality, perseverance—the cry of *gambatte!* We can learn to improve products and reduce deficits. But can we learn to cross cultures and make the world a better place? If I were a thoughtful young Japanese, I would ask myself: What does Japan really stand for in the world? What has it to offer the global community, beyond superior technology and consumer goods? Why do so many people around the globe speak English rather than Japanese? Is it only because Japan lost the war? Only the Japanese, only the young Japanese, can really answer that challenge.

But what can present America contribute to transcultural values, to making the world a better place? Export McDonald's, Madonna, Disney World, and the Terminator? Export the right of anyone to sue everyone or infect them with AIDS? It's hardly what the world needs. Yet in the past, even before Jefferson's "pursuit of happiness," America itself has served as an experiment in transcultural values, an experiment in which American colleges gradually became key. Is the experiment failing? Has America betrayed its best self? Can it overcome its current crisis of social trust and emerge stronger, as James Fallows put it, not more like Japan but "more like us?" These questions, again, remain in youth's keeping, American youth.

So let me conclude with two anecdotes of youth.

In the fall of 1989, Iwao Iwamoto and I taught an honors seminar at my university on Contemporary American and Japanese Fiction (we called it "The Eagle and the Rising Sun"). One of the most eager students in that seminar was Mark Zimmerman, a gentle, lumbering giant with reddish blond hair receding from a massive pate and round eyes made rounder by his granny glasses, forever staring at the world in poetic surprise. Mark liked the course, liked the reading—he even liked his teachers. He applied for a JET (Japanese English-Teaching) fellowship. To his astonishment and delight, he found himself in Japan. He wrote me a letter from which I excerpt:

I'm living in the town of Ikuno (pop. 5,000), about 80 km SW of Osaka. It's a very quiet and serene locale, almost sleepy. If not for the train station here you could call it remote as well. Ikuno lies in a narrow river valley that winds through the Chugoku mountain range. The mountains are dominant and their terrain resembles that of the Shenandoahs. At night you hear one of two things: crickets or rain. The sky gets dead black too, revealing dim stars. There are also many Buddha statues and Coke machines here.

During the week I teach fourteen classes at Ikuno Junior High School, six of them with Ms. Hirata and eight with Ms. Etani. Neither of them is fluent, but if they were I probably wouldn't be here. Both of them work hard, though, and seem eager to improve their English. Many of the students are also geared up for English so I think it will be a productive year in the classroom. So far so good. . . .

At times, though, it's really strange being the local blond. The reception's been mixed. I've had little kids run off at the sight of me while others, believe it or not, ask me for my autograph. I have to admit that I really enjoy signing autographs—so far no-one's been turned away. Other times people come up to me and tug or stroke my hair, a rather creepy experience at first. Pretty soon, though, I'll be old hat and then we can get down to more substantial contacts. We have some interesting things to talk about—a good incentive for me to learn as much Japanese as I can.

Here are all the elements of cultural translation—and some elements of mistranslation too. Both kinds inform my next anecdote.

I once asked another student, Isono, if she was building bridges between our cultures, our countries. "Bridges?" she said doubtfully. "I'm not building bridges. Older people have already built them, after the war." She paused. "I think young people today easily exchange cultures, move between countries, without guilt."

I thought, really? If so, then in planetary insouciance may lie the seeds of transcultural values. But when I relayed the story to an older Japanese colleague, he firmly said, "That young lady has selfish ideas," and changed the subject. His resistance is not only "Japanese"; it is part of the world's history, that part some live to overcome, and all must overcome to live. It is also the part that the poet, Makoto Ooka, tries to overcome in his linked verse, linked across continents.

MAKOTO OOKA

Roundness and zest—that was my first impression of him. A small, ki-netic man, ready with laughter, intellectually benevolent. Later, when I read his poetry, I understood better his sunny, no, his cosmic charm.

Sally and I met him first at a party given by Mrs. Tsutsumi. As Kanzaki Seijo, she had entranced us, performing a series of slow, circling, Jiuta-Mai dances in the Nihonbashi Mitsukoshi Auditorium. Later, she in-vited her guests to a supper at Rain Tree. Still rapt with that poignant delicacy of motion—Jiuta-Mai dances often tell sad stories of love from a woman's perspective—we joined the conversation slowly, reluctantly. Ooka drew us into the postperformance celebration.

He spoke of the "countertradition" in Japanese culture: not Bud-dhism, Confucianism, the fastidiousness of aristocrats, the austerity of samurai, but the raucous, sometimes raffish, always colorful and earthy popular tradition as it affected Japanese arts. He spoke fluently, stopping to listen, cocking his head, speaking again, at once delightful and self-delighting. Without knowing anything about him then, I thought: here is a man basking innocently in the warmth of his creative energies.

Ooka is prolific beyond the limits of decency. More than 150 vol-umes of poetry, essays, translations, lectures, editions, treatises on paint-ing, daily critiques of poetry, ancient and modern, in the *Asahi Shimbun*, accumulating prizes. Yet the man remains modest, ebullient, running smoothly along "the axial lines of existence," as Augie March might say.

Axial lines, yes, but also circumferences—they matter. Culture in Japan, we saw, is decentered; the self is not its core. Poetry, for instance, reveals a constant tension, Ooka argues in *The Colors of Poetry*, between *utage*, the communal banquet, and *koshin*, the solitary mind, a tension which at its high points defines the history of Japanese poetry. Thus Ooka: "What I find extremely interesting is that only those poets who are aware of the 'solitary mind' and remain faithful to their personal fate…while keeping a place within the 'banquet,' only those poets produce works at which we stare in wonder." Works that Ooka himself has produced.

The enormous number of Japanese who still join tanka or haiku associations, join calligraphy, tea ceremony, and flower-arranging clubs, may aspire to transform quotidian life into art. But the aspiration of Ooka, I sense, is different: it is to mediate between tradition and experiment, Japan and the West, universal experience and the personal voice. A demanding act, a complex fate. As Ooka admits in his address to the forty-seventh International PEN Congress in Tokyo (1984): "Although I was brought up immersed in the Japanese tradition, I am also a modern poet and, whether I like it or not, have a Western sense of self-consciousness in the heart of my creative consciousness."

Hence Ooka's assays in linked verse, *renga* and *renku*, with both Japanese and non-Japanese poets like Thomas Fitzsimmons (see the collaborative volume, *Linked Poems: Rocking Mirror Daybreak* [1987]). *Renga*, Ooka once told me, may encapsulate the high paradox of Japan itself: the elimination of self-concern for the sake of true individuality. I wondered to myself: high paradox or wishful hope?

In contemporary Japanese life, I saw mainly the coercive, the ener-
vating side of the paradox; happy resolutions belonged to sainthood
or national myths. But in Ooka's person I perceived a genial embodi-
ment of Japanese contradictions turned into art. No, there was something there beyond contradictions, other than "art." A radiant sensuality
perhaps—for Ooka, women and imagination are one, as Wallace
Stevens failed to say. Or a mystic, a unitary, intuition of words and
things, as in the opening lines of "Words/Words":

> I keep
> on a vacant lot
> an invisible horse,
> ride off sometimes to see
> a 12th century Zen priest—
> after 800 years
> his body's gone,
> turned into words.

(About the thirteenth-century Zen master, Dogen, Ooka also said:
"Here there exists an absolute universe of expression in which words
do not express things; rather, things express themselves as words.") Or
perhaps there was in him a quality of impersonal, unillusioned repose,
a quality that drew me repeatedly to Japan. Here is a section of "Let
Mt. Fuji Lay Eggs":

> Above the trail
> a haze of light comes drifting
> from the farthest reaches of the universe.

Water fleas in the west,
plankton in the east,
mayflies in the south—

they forever
lead their brief lives
in the universe's drifting light.

They tell us, "When you die, die,
with no complaint, no sentimentality.
That's the way to live fully!"

But where had this ideal Japan hidden in the country I actually visit and revisit? I began to construct for myself a personal dictionary of Japanese culture, hoping to find among its brusque entries my own sympathies and antipathies, some clues of its presence.

PART V
ENTRIES, A TO Z

JAPANESE CULTURE:
A PERSONAL DICTIONARY

APOLOGY

Ambiguous. Ambiguous, like so many things Japanese.

A politician may say something outrageous—about American laziness or blacks, for instance—then simulate an apology only to reinforce the original statement. But a samurai, occasionally a company president, may apologize with his life. From cynicism to seppuku, the ultimate "sincere" act.

The art of apology: to observe the form, recant without necessary contrition. It is also the way to break through a double bind.

Example? A Japanese student, scheduled to give an oral report on a certain day, absents himself. Next week, he comes to my office. He does not lie: I was sick, my mother died. No, he bows deeply and says, "Sorry, very sorry." The end. Only a foreigner or a cad would pursue the matter with this student further.

Explanation? The student thinks: I can't possibly give that report in English, I can't possibly fail to appear on the day of my report. Nigeru-ki (avoidance) and giri (duty) collide. Intolerable dilemma. Deep apology. Very sorry.

But let us not be cynical. To a "sincere" Japanese—and most strive to be so—apology means loss of face, shame. This is painful. What will my family, my friends, say? The feeling is interiorized, just as Freudian guilt is a parent interiorized. Then it becomes *giri* toward oneself, toward one's name, akin to honor, dignity, pride. This makes for unusual sensitivity to criticism or detraction—just as in many Third World cultures?

The corruption of apology: a high ideal used meanly, a fiction of contrition without atonement, those politicians exploiting the intrinsic ambiguity—Westerners say no, no, it's hypocrisy—of Japanese culture. (See, later, under War Crimes.) But apologies, like some clear, fragrant oil, also lubricate that culture.

BOREDOM

They seem sometimes bored, sleepy, listless. *Pachinko* parlors; trains like traveling dorms; eyes closed in hotel lobbies, in lecture halls; off duty, a slow, shuffling walk—is it the habit of slippers?

Some say, "They work hard. They are tired. They seek serenity." Others reply, "They have no broad interests—oh, yes, golf—no inner resources." Some say, "They value silence, economy of feeling, and gesture." Others reply, "Their secret is lassitude."

Ruth Benedict: "When the Japanese have a vision of a great mission they lose their boredom. They lose it completely and absolutely, no matter how distant the goal. Their particular kind of ennui is the sickness of an over-vulnerable people." And of an overachieving people.

Boredom, then, as the other face of anxiety, energy, ambition. We know about the energy, the ambition. The anxiety of these "impassive" people is special. I have seen young men, always men, sweat profusely, imperturbably, in a tense moment—say, before the boss. They feel acutely self-conscious, which means conscious of another. They think, am I behaving well? Have I said anything wrong? Did I do the job perfectly? This is no ordinary anxiety. Call it the habit of meticulousness, call it terror of disapprobation. They meet in the bone.

Boredom, then, may come as surcease from the quest for perfection. Like the flaw in a Japanese vase, like Zen foolery or Chinese drunken boxing. A kind of evasion. A way of staying spiritually alive, if a little numb. A sort of hiding, waiting, waiting for an experience genuinely your own.

Once I saw a young matron on a bench in Yoyogi Park. She watched the Elvis look-alike tribes slouch around—studded leather jackets, pointy shoes, forelocks resting on nose tip—cluster in small circles, break into frantic rock and roll. She yawned. She is not sleepy, I thought; she longs for something neither fashion nor history can give her in Japan.

CLEANLINESS

Godliness is next to cleanliness in Japan—all the gods bathed together after their labor of creation. Actually, godliness comes quite a bit farther down the line.

Taxi drivers with spotless white gloves; unblemished toilets; immaculate kitchens; a new toothbrush every day in hotels; wood, tile, steel, cloth, scrubbed till each yields its inmost self to the user.

I once spent a jet-lagged morning in the small town of Futtsu, watching—yes, I know, it's rude, ruder still in Japan—watching my neighbor's wife scrub the day. Clad in a zebra top and white slacks, she began with the family Honda. Wash, rinse, wash, dry, polish, till the car became incandescent blue. Then she did the laundry and hung it out to dry, dry and flap like angels in the wind. The windows came next. Wash, wipe, buff. She clambered out of a window onto the roof of the kitchen to do one set. She did the glass panes, the wire screens, the shoji. Her energy seemed boundless, her domestic virtue manifest. She moved rapidly, gracefully, with a will. By 10 AM, I felt exhausted, and returned to bed for a nap.

Cleanliness: more discipline than hygiene, an exercise in scruple, a kind of asceticism, the discharge of a responsibility (I'm doing my bit for others). It is really what every successful society needs. "Not like those countries," Sally says, "that have the Bomb but undrinkable tap water."

Not that Japan is consistently hygienic. The odor of sewage rises from country ditches, from fields, rises even from some city streets. Old houses rely on outhouses—40 percent of Japanese households have no access to sewers. Hepatitis remains a hazard. But there is a zany charm, which quickly waned for me, in taking off shoes, putting on slippers, to enter a house; taking off slippers to step into a tatami room; exchanging one kind of slippers for another to use the toilet; exchanging slippers for wooden clogs to take a bath. It's all ritualistic, not realistic, magic, not science. Collective ablutions in public baths, hot springs everywhere, thriving Thalassal resorts. Cleanliness as sacrament and communion.

And look at the money. Feel those crisp, clean bills, never smudged, creased, tattered. Do they print them every hour on the hour? Freud identified gold with feces. In Japan, money seems more ambiguous. It never goes directly from hand to hand in public places; it passes on a tray, atop a receipt. Or wrapped in lovely noshigami (red, white, and yes, gold) as a present. Such fastidiousness! How else treat "filthy lucre"?

Cleanliness: I feel it in Japan as solidarity, collective ascesis, not the faltering individual will of a once-Protestant ethic, not the clamorous, divisive ethos of modern Islam. But I feel it, too, as displaced obsession, an archaic memory of disorder and dearth.

Futtsu again, the beach. Black-and-slate volcanic sand, flotsam, jetsam, refuse everywhere, washed ashore from Tokyo Bay. Shacks and lean-tos straggling the dunes; scrub, bulrush, bamboo, swaying in the air. The waters of the bay and a listless estuary brown, brackish; a scraggy jetty prods the waters. On one side, the hills rise, wooded, drab green. A lonely vista, elusive grandeur and desolation; nature marred, scarred, somehow a touch of sublimity. . . . An old woman appears on the empty beach. White apron and hood and a peasant's false sleeves. She rakes the sand continuously, burning the refuse in a fire behind her; the smoke drifts, gray against the horizon. She rakes tirelessly, gathering, piling, burning. She is all purpose, gristle.

Iwamoto is with me. He speaks with her. Her house burned in the war. She moved out here, to a cabin behind the scrubby hillocks. The sand drifts into her cabin, she sweeps it out ceaselessly. Another Woman of the Dunes. And while she is at it, she scours, rakes, cleans her part of the beach, burning the refuse from Tokyo Bay—from the whole world.

DEPARTMENT STORES

The best emporia on earth. Seibu, Mitsukoshi, Takashimaya, Marui, Matsuya, Matsuzakaya, Isetan, Jusco, Sogo, Hankyu, Odakyu, Daimaru—upmarket, downmarket. Varied, ingenious, inclusive, courteous to a fault. And exorbitant, for dollar spenders at least. I think of them as fleets of consumer dreams, with proud flagships—Seibu in Ikebukuro, Mitsukoshi in Nihonbashi, etc.

What makes the *depatos* special? First, a delirium of consumerism, a frenzy of fashions. Superproducers, the Japanese try to recycle their wealth by becoming superconsumers—try in vain. Second, unimaginably dense cities, human needs, desires, urgencies, impacted in every square mile of the urban landscape.

Third, a gift culture (see Gifts), dedicated to the exchange of symbolic objects. Fourth, a kind of naïveté or credulity, tolerance of media hype, a willing suspension of disbelief in advertising—a sort of mass poesis. Fifth, besides shopping, what else is there to do? TV, golf? In fact, TV and shopping are symbiotic: one consumes time, the other money, goods that the former flaunts. And golf? Mostly men golf, women shop, and golfing costs more than shopping anyway.

Oh, I know: consumerism satisfies needs deeper than we admit. But when it becomes the main praxis of a society, something there becomes permanently glazed. In Japan, a Department Store Culture—like our Mall Cultures?—has taken hold. A whole generation, growing up within it, knows little beside it. Its glamour pervades childhood fantasies, an alternate fairyland.

And why not? Take Seibu. Together with its satellites in the Saison Corporation—Parco, In the Room, Wave, SMA, Seed, Loft—it offers concerts, art galleries, dance recitals, vocational schools, insurance policies, holiday tours, golf ranges, bowling alleys, vacation resorts, banks, theater agencies, interior decorators, personal advice—plus, of course, every conceivable merchandise. All the services, all the goods. And when something goes wrong, an employee appears at your doorstep to apologize, explain, rectify.

The department store as urban cornucopia, a heterocosm, which we enter to lose ourselves. Better than *pachinko* parlors. A utopia—or is it dystopia?—nearly achieved.

ECONOMY

Here the clichés crowd: "Japan, Inc.," "Japanese, the Economic Animals," "Keep those transistor salesmen away from me" (De-Gaulle). We hear that Japan has no foreign policy, only an eco-

nomic interest; that its system of layered distributors and inter-
locking keiretsu favors producers, not consumers; that it protects
fanatically at home, dumps implacably abroad. Prices? A bottle of
Jack Daniels in Osaka costs four times what a bottle of Suntory
Royal costs in Chicago; a steak dinner of Kobe or Matsuzaka
beef—don't even think about it. And the price of rice, mystic
staple of the land? Please!

All clichés, you say? Certainly, and they ring both true and
false, as clichés do. Meantime, the prodigious trade balances ac-
crue—and the prodigious irritations. Not only Edith Cresson exclaims with typical Gallic spleen: "Ces fourmis!" Other nations
fumble economically and fume.

The Japanese, I have said, retain an acute sense of dearth that
intimates disorder. Memories of the Pacific war exacerbate that
awareness. And who knows what new shokku awaits them around
the corner of history? How, then, can enough ever seem enough
to them? How can they not, eleven years after the war, lead the
world in steel industries, and two decades after, lead in transis-
tors, robotry, banking, advertising? Proud and half resentful—
perpetually so since the Meiji Restoration—they saw on their
postwar movie screens images of a glittering, enfabled America
and vowed, as the filmmaker Nagisa Oshima says, to surpass them.

Yet I do not believe the Japanese value money as much as Chinese or Americans do. In the seventeenth century, a famous bowl
exceeded a castle in worth; a famous sword was priceless. About
the labor value of an old garment, Tokugawa Ieyasu said, "If we
do not think, while using things, of the time and effort re-
quired to make them—then our want of consideration puts us
on a level with the beasts."

Wealth, mercantilism, as prime values in Japan? I think not.
Rather, national survival, to which economic effort is only a

means, a dismal means. Economy, economics, the dismal science, the science of dearth. The radical effort to survive. Has it gone berserk in Japan? Anything to stave off disorder.

FAX (See *also* Urbanism)

Suddenly, all the *meishi* (name cards) had fax numbers. My friends in Tokyo would ask, "What is your fax?" I was living in Tokyo myself, practically next door. I was not a business. Why should I have a fax? But the gadget began to tease my mind. After all, I had written about a semiotic, intercommunicative earth nearly two decades ago. I bought a fax machine.

A print rather than an aural freak, I love the smart, warbling thing. I would rather fax than phone. Formality and immediacy, the thoughtfulness of writing at (almost) light speed, electrons inspiriting an old-fashioned machine. McLuhan synthesized.

It was another Scot, Alexander Bain (1810–1878), who patented the process in 1843—a century and a half ago, a decade before Perry anchored in Tokyo Bay. In 1865, three years before the Emperor Meiji ascended the throne, a protofax, called *le pan-télégraphe*, linked Paris to Lyon. It was not a success. French, German, British, Italian, American engineers tinkered for a century with the contraption. In 1974, digital fax appeared in America. But someone dropped the ball. Then, in the early eighties, the Japanese picked it up and scored and scored and scored. Try buying today an American fax machine.

There are more than two thousand characters in the Japanese language. Who can squeeze them all through a teleprinter? The Japanese adopted the digital process. They miniaturized. They had the microchips, the fastidious technology. They can put 39,788 facsimile "squares" of light in an inch square. And now the machines beep and "shake hands" across the world.

Miniaturization—Bucky Fuller's "ephemeralization"—doing more with less. I called it the new gnosticism. A layer of language, not matter but mind, now envelops the earth. Something like Teilhard's noosphere. Japan, a gnostic nation; Tokyo, a gnostic city. Knowledge at a premium, information everywhere in the air. The constant, silent slither of electric signals fills space. Signs, symbols, emblems saturate the culture, connecting it to its future and past.

Take Tokyo, fax city. It is not a pretty town—in most hotels, the higher the floor, the uglier the view. The city is a labyrinth, full of dead ends, absent signs, vanishing streets—only *chos* (quarters) and *chomes* (blocks) to guide you. Taxi drivers rarely know their destination. The maps are oriented in every cardinal direction, not only due north. Residents shamefacedly admit they cannot guide you to a shop in an adjacent block. The traffic jams boggle time.

Or take Shinjuku, Tokyo's microcosm: clumps of love hotels, swarms of bars, jumbles of restaurants, bookshops, offices, department stores, back alleys, a thin strip of bamboo garden, a rivulet, and suddenly—where did it come from?—a vast temple. No wonder Ridley Scott found in Shinjuku, not in some imaginary Los Angeles, his model for *Blade Runner*. There is no center in Tokyo, some say, only an emptiness, the emperor's invisible palace, the emperor himself, phantom of power.

Tokyo is pastiche, collage, a theme park, a postmodern city, everyone says. I go further: I think of Tokyo as a gigantic brain, all software and circuitry, perpetually reinventing, reconstituting its patterns, with pockets of noise, entropy, forgetfulness here and there. How else communicate, then, within that brain— soon the whole earth—except by fax, cordless phone, computer, satellite?

Yes, thanks to the Japanese practical genius, Camille Paglia and Julie Burchill can now insult one another by fax.

GIFTS

They bind. Ligaments, membranes, lymphs, flowing blood join-
ing all the cells. Gifts bind Japan in a body of infinitely quali-
fied, ever-renewed obligations. A body of signs, really.

The Chinook practice of potlatch, or *patshatl*, served as an archaic ritual of both status and reciprocity. In Japan, the practice
suggests something primal but also finely calibrated. Its economy
blends art, morality, politics, eroticism, semiotics—the gift itself,
as use value, vanishes into the sign. But in Zen, ownership is
ugly, objects circulate, circulate in the space of *mu*, the void.

At first sight, though, the practice seems sometimes absurd.

Item: I lectured once at a university near Christmastime. A
junior professor there, whom I barely knew, offered me shyly a
gift, a silk tie, very *shibui*. I asked my host, "Why does Morita
give me this tie?" He unhesitatingly replied, "Because he is Japanese."

Item: a soup can the size of a large thimble, from the Okura
Hotel gift shop, sells at a preposterously high price. The label,
the sign, matters; the soup doesn't. The label makes the giver's
point. At the Okura, they can barely keep up with the demand.

Item: neighbors and friends came to the funeral of a man we
know, bringing money or flowers. Seven weeks later, his widow
went to a special department in Takashimaya and bought eighty-
three presents for each and all. The store sent them with appro-
priate—that is, formulaic—notes.

Item: a catalog listing thousands of gifts—their relative values,
proper occasions, etiquette of wrapping, giving, reciprocation—
remains an enduring best-seller in Japan.

Gifts, not bribes, form the basis of relationships. (Is the basis
in America money, in Egypt bribes, rhetoric?) Gifts in Japan,
though, move laterally or upwards, rarely downwards. Men of
status bestow favors, receive gifts.

For me, who actually dislikes presents, the glory of Japanese gifts is their wrappings. They express care, devotion, but also distance. They mediate between the giver, the gift, the recipient. They promise delay, they heighten; like art, they both conceal and reveal. Indeed, they are aesthetic objects in themselves; gifts enclosing gifts or without gifts. Call them disposable signifiers, no less gravid for that.

No wonder that stores take such pains to design their wrappers—originally, the festive *noshigami* was made of thinly pressed abalone—and pains to wrap gifts (crisp edges, neat, flat ribbons, patterns that recall the art of origami).

Do the Japanese, then, wrap for wrapping's sake? Not really. Except for their government, which always gives too little, too late, they never skimp in hospitality or presents. Their forms may seem hollow, their hearts are rarely empty.

HUMOR

The less said, the better: the Japanese are not reputed for their humor. They had to borrow a word for it, *yumoa*.

But also how overlook it? Their tradition reaches back to the raunchy laughter of gods, to untrammeled fertility cults and village carnivals, to the farcical Kyogen, relieving No drama as satyr plays once relieved Greek tragedy. This earthy tradition lives on in countless stories told in bars, schoolrooms, offices, *ryokans*, lives even in the scabrous *manga*. A collective heritage of Shinto animism and bawdy love. Did not Light (Amaterasu) return to the world because the Dread Female of Heaven performed her lascivious dance before the howling, approving gods?

Yes, eroticism and humor are kin. Not only in the ancient *matsuri* festivals. Also in Heian courtly dalliance, the sophisticated wit of geisha, the sexual banter of the *mizu shobai* in the Yoshiwara pleasure quarter of Edo.

Then, of course, there is the sly, metaphysical laughter of Zen Buddhism, both resonant and still, an infinite echo the other side of banality.

Why, then, do I miss high humor in Japan? Smiles, yes, and good cheer, and sometimes raffish jokes or archaic pranks. But quotidian humor, requiring thought, irony, a wry sense of contradiction? Perhaps the Japanese are too polite, perhaps too sincere. They are certainly averse to teasing, which puzzles them first and irritates them last. Is it not an attack on their dignity, they wonder? Or at least a breach of propriety? Only old friends tease in Japan, and even then tease gingerly. Everyone owes it to himself—yes, it's rather male—to be taken seriously. Dignity, giri toward oneself.

Girls, of course, giggle, covering their mouth daintily with a hand. That's femininity, winsome manners. But humor?

There is, as we have seen, a powerful tension between an autochthonous culture in Japan and overlays of Buddhist pessimism, Confucian puritanism, Tokugawa vigilance. The old popular culture can still erupt in vaudeville, slapstick, grotesque humor; in parodies of "Stupid Dad" (a comic book series) and pathetic salarymen, called fondly by their wives "oversize trash"; in television commercials of nearly demented zaniness; in pornography, much of it vicious, some of it artful.

I sense that tension, particularly when it snaps, and a group of decorous academics, say, begins to act a bit obscenely, a little childishly. With their new affluence, Ian Buruma thinks, the Japanese are beginning to expose their raucous side—hoping still that it will escape the gaijin's prim eye.

I

Yes, I, who carps and cavils here. Who? Why?

The Japanese avoid *watakushi*, the first-person pronoun, if they can, and often anglicize the possessive, saying mai. I—see?—intersperse this book with the pronoun, hoping to exchange an I for an eye. Hoping to observe more candidly, more sharply, through self-observation, through self-implication. In other words, it's not just "them."

But what had I finally to do with Japan? I never fell in love with a woman there—Eros takes us to a nation's heart—or spent my green youth by Fuji's side. In fairness, though, neither did I wish to distance myself from this far land, sensing affinities with it that I never felt on native ground.

What, then, drew me to Japan? The idea of a culture so different from one I never chose (Egypt), and different still from another I chose even before seeing (America)? Was it a quest for wholeness or perfection, trying to find between America and Japan the Ideal Place? To such a place, to such a culture, could one aspire, discovering in its highest promise (America?) and its highest exaction (Japan?) relief on a disappointed earth?

Such a place, of course, could never be, and if it existed, could only be found within. The "disappointed earth" (Egypt?) may be our lasting inheritance. But it is an inheritance, I do believe, that we are free to recreate.

Hence the Japanese. "Them": they are not exactly US, rather a part of my aspiring self. This makes for asperity sometimes, a tartness in the blood. Blood? I mean the plasma of dreams.

JAPLISH

Some say that the Japanese language has become a kind of pidgin. Indeed. But there is another view. "If English were for sale," writes Waka Tsunoda, "the United States would have no trade deficit with Japan"—perhaps even, I would add, a garrulous surplus.

English infiltrates scientific journals, national weeklies, fashion magazines. It also enters Japanese literature, as in Ryu Mu-rakami's *Almost Transparent Blue*, which won the Akutagawa Prize in 1976, and Yasuo Tanaka's *Somehow, Crystal*, which won the Bungei Prize in 1980. And even when English forgets itself in Japan, it leaves behind a musical trace: one of the most popular songs is "Auld Lang Syne," renamed "Hotaru no Hikari" (The Light of the Firefly), sung to Japanese lyrics.

This interaction between languages can sometimes seem odd to native speakers. Few Americans, for instance, would be happy to drink Pocari Sweat (actually a tasty soft drink) or mix Creap (powdered milk) with their coffee. A Tokyo ad in English, fea-turing a Caucasian model wearing a three-piece suit, reads: "For men who live on 'Now.' Hot Mind Tailored." Another ad for a laundry: "Hi-Sense Cleaning." A T-shirt reads: "Height is Shin-ing"; a black leather jacket: "I Like Mother Fuckers"; a lady's bag: "Elle de Elle—for Innocent Women"; a bakery shopping bag: "Scandinavia Natural Roman: Best Bread Message"; and a hotel wedding service brags: "Fantastic and Open."

Obviously, the Japanese often use foreign words like free-float-ing signifiers, meaning anything, unless the letter *o* or *u* is tacked at the end of the word, as in *aisu-kuriimu, happi-endo, faito* (fight), *tafu* (tough), *kissu, rabu hoteru* (love hotel), *tarento, feminisuto*, which Japanizes the word, turning it into "real" language; then the Japanese use the word, as if it had sprung from Yamato earth.

Such verbal appropriations, *gairaigo*, are not always ludicrous. They may indicate linguistic curiosity—contrast with French prissiness about their language—and at the same time a form of transcultural vitality, an exchange of global energies that the fu-ture cannot rescind. They may also show verve and ingenuity: *moga* (contraction of modern girl), *sobaju* (*sauvage* hairdo), TPO (appropriateness to Time, Place, Occasion), *sebiro* (Saville Row, or any three-piece suit), *batakusai* (smelling of butter, said of a

Japanese too Westernized), *no-ka-de* (no car day, or prohibited traffic).

Obviously, shockingly, Furizu! has not yet entered the Japanese vocabulary, resulting in the shooting of Yoshihiro Hattori, a foreign exchange student in Baton Rouge, when he failed to obey the command. But Japanese TV shows, like "Kyosen's Unusable English," together with private seminars on "Defensive English," serve as national survival courses for Japanese tourists whose school English—six years of it—lends itself so readily to parody and tragedy.

Yes, Japlish twists and turns. A "mansion" in London or New York is not an apartment house in Tokyo. And "freeze" in street language involves no temperature drop. But the comment of Hiroshi Kume, anchor of TV-Asahi, must haunt us all: "It is said that the ready acceptance of guns in America is just the result of a cultural difference. But over there—how can you call it a culture?"

Put it more broadly: what exactly does English disseminate in the world? Democracy, dollars, technology, death?

KITSCH, ETC.

Kitsch, camp, cuteness, vulgarity, sentimentality, cheap imitation. What a postmodern salmagundi. Who can theorize it?

Item: Café Opéra in fashionable Azabu, Tokyo. A grand auditorium, complete with stage curtains, dimmed chandeliers, gilded columns, velvet armchairs, famous arias spilling from the audio system, a place exorbitant and unreal. An Occidental there may feel parodied until he realizes that the ethos of the "café" is both campily celebratory and dazzlingly naive. Or take Caffe Bongo, about which Charles Jencks says, "Post-Holocaust design celebrates the warped destruction of high-tech in a baroque frenzy, or plays it very sombre and cool."

Item: The "Palacio" dining hall of the Toya Park Hotel in Hokkaido. Empire lustres; Chagall-like stained-glass windows three stories high; Ionian columns supporting a false arbor against one wall; a half-roof of terra-cotta tiles, hacienda style; a stage with a pink, mechanical piano worthy of Liberace at the center; a "Viking Smorgasboard" groaning with Japanese, Chinese, and Occidental dishes; a clientele ranging from old Hokkaido farmers to schoolboys and -girls in prim English blazers, up from elite Tokyo schools, and the ubiquitous honeymooners.

Item: Japanese businessmen tour the English countryside in a Bentley, searching for the perfect Tudor village. They plan to erect a replica, ninety miles outside of Tokyo, to help Japanese students learn English in a suitable ambiance. Unlike the original, though, this village will be built to withstand earthquakes, nine points on the Richter scale. Cost? A trifling £25 million.

Item: At gas stations, mechanical pandas or life-size dolls flag down motorists, inviting them to fill up. In the kitchen of a friend, a musical clock, singing Beatles songs on the hour, and "Happy Birthday to You" on family birthdays. In the picture windows of fashionable "mansions," all manner of small, soft, cute, cuddly, furry or feathery things—bunnies and squirrels, kiwis and canaries, big-eyed bambis of every species.

Item: A late-night television program called "Banana Chips Love." The famous statue of U.S. Marines raising the flag on Iwo Jima advertises a product. What? A narrative sequence incomprehensible in either English or Japanese, muted voices, fragmented scenes. The ad and story sequences blend into one another. Brilliant colors, graphics, editing, absurdism. See also Kenchi Iwamoto's bizarre film on "human discommunication," *Monkeys in Paradise*. The director has been slickly called a "hallucinating Japanese Woody Allen."

Item: Between Christmas and New Year's, Beethoven's Ninth

Symphony reverberates from one end of the archipelago to the other. In the Kanto region alone, 1,300 performances. The full symphony, including the plangent "Ode to Joy": "*Alle Menschen werden Brüder.*" Really? An old Japanese credo?

Item: A new fashion among young men: a full-body, *Yakuza*-style tatoo. Beyond mod or punk, Sagi's stylish simulations of the dread gangster's skin. But with Occidental images, pleasing patterns. Still, tattooed yuppies may be denied access to fashionable swimming pools lest they frighten other bathers away.

Item: A post Bubble, bubble-gum-chewing junior geisha, called Hana. While awaiting her "sponsor" to become a full geisha, she writes comic books—with a space-cadet geisha heroine—computer games, pop music; she conducts a band; she insists that David Bowie shares her birthday, "the only man to whom she wants to give up her virginity."

Item: The Bodi-con (body-consciousness) girls, OLs (office ladies) by day, nocturnal vamps at discos like Juliana. Lacroix and Lagerfeld now passé, new microminis instead, with SM spike heels and outré accessories to bedizen the body, befuddle the consciousness. Sexiness as playful, trendy showiness. The gonads going PoMo. Look but Do Not Touch. When a *wan-lenguzu bodicon garu* (the real McCoy) walks, her various bangles go *chara-chara*.

The *bumu* (booms, fads, waves) break, one after the other, on the shores of kitsch. Or is it fair to call it all postmodern kitsch? Certainly no Unified Theory of recent Japanese culture will satisfy. Though the country remains an imploded, conformist society, its cities, particularly Tokyo, have bred a headlong variety of pop and youthful subcultures. The Bubble of (continuing) affluence helped. So did the Japanese proneness to fashions, to appropriation without regard to "authenticity" or "origins." Call it dynamic promiscuity, call it a genius for mimesis—Japanese signs were liberated long before Barthes or Derrida.

If kitsch, then this is kitsch of a special kind. The parody is often unconscious, the irony frequently unintended, the allusion almost forgotten. There is glossiness, the high-tech flatness of postmodernism, yes. There is ignorance, cheapening, vulgarity, too. There is idiocy. But even these, in their prodigal if finally controlled variousness, manifest awesome vitality.

But what of this unexpected cuteness, sentimentality—a kind of sugary rot? In the land of pitiless samurai, colonists, industrialists, pornographers? Well, even the TV samurai soap operas have become syrupy. Is it the feminization—largely a positive feature—of Japanese culture, a kind of postmodern Heian return? Is it the mother cult, a recovery of childhood? A compensation for the rigors of Japanese existence, all study and work, so little romance, so much pragmatism? An extension, perhaps perversion, of sociability and tact, the need to eliminate sharp edges—we have no corners, the Japanese boast—from human intercourse? The obverse of violence, as in some parts of German or American life?

Whatever its causes, its effects cloy. The hyperfeminine manners of the traditional Japanese woman become in her liberated granddaughter at best quaint, at worst sham, a preposterous tic. Cuteness meets kitsch.

LAW (See *also* Order)

There are few law societies in the world; Japan is not among them. Societies are more efficiently ruled, the Grand Inquisitor would claim, by Miracle, Mystery, and Authority. A Japanese may call them Ritual, Custom, and Consensus. Smiling thinly, the Inquisitor would nod.

Japanese politicians break the law routinely, cabinet ministers defy the supreme court of the land. Except for certain show trials—of Kakuei Tanaka, say, or Shin Kanemaru—scoundrels in power go scot-free, at worst receive a slap on the wrist. For other mortals, indictment means conviction, if seldom jail. The rate of conviction for major crimes, nearly 99 percent, makes American law enforcers glow green with envy.

In Japan, Authority, not the Law, is respected. Hence the regard for policemen, not lawyers. The latter have no reason to strut. In a homogeneous, conforming society, conflict is either mediated or shunned. Courts become institutions of final, not first, resort. Once a case reaches court, judges tend to apportion blame somewhat evenly between litigants. Who is completely right, entirely wrong? And if people permit themselves to appear in court, is this not proof they are all to blame?

I once asked a top Osaka lawyer about the virtual absence of the jury system in Japan. "It wouldn't work," he joked. "The Japanese take too much time to decide. They won't decide where another authority can. And if they decide, they want always to acquit. Anyway, we are not a very logical people."

No inconsistencies here. The urge is to avoid both confrontation and personal blame. Instead: courtesy, forbearance, a sweet feeling for order, sacrifice.

Consider the *koban* (police boxes in every city quarter). They help residents and strangers alike. Unstintingly, ungrudgingly. *Koban* also know everything, quietly watch. One day, when we were living in Tokyo, a policeman paid us a visit. He was small, trim, courteous in a pixie way, and fully armed. He spoke twenty words of English. But his intent was unmistakable. Sorry, very sorry to trouble. Would honorable residents fill out this form? Please to register. Police want to assist. Everyone bowing, smiling. He left, waving goodbye to Sally through the kitchen window. It was all so genial, almost seductive.

The police as seduction. Good order as politesse, self-discipline, a lack of insistence on self. Things fall quietly into place. Almost a dream—until it turns into a nightmare.

MARRIAGE

Think of Japanese marriage, think of women. They are in charge of things connubial. Not chattel, if ever they were. After all, they are quick to remind you, this is the land of Lady Murasaki; of Sei Shonagon, author of the brilliant, eleventh-century *Pillow Book*; of Takako Doi, former leader of the opposition Socialist Party; of the eternally popular play, *Mother Behind My Eyes*; of Sadako Ogata, United Nations High Commissioner for Refugees; and now of the *sogoshoku*, the rising career woman.

Young women have become demanding, men complain. The *omiai* (matchmaker) may still be around, but nubile women now insist on the "Three Highs": high stature, high education, high income—ideally, a tall, handsome, Todai engineer. With the influx of foreign labor, the young men have also become choosy, avoiding difficult, dirty, and dangerous jobs: call it the "Three Lows."

The New Women marry later or not at all (*shinguru uman*), have fewer children, divorce more frequently than their mothers, who are catching up by divorcing their husbands after retirement— bothersome men, clinging to doorsteps, the expression goes, like wet leaves. Young or old, the women have begun to move into the world. They found or join consumer and activist groups. I wonder again: a Velvet Revolution? Well, they may have helped force the resignation of three prime ministers in the last decade and altered the patterns of work and leisure permanently in the nation.

Till recently, the Japanese marriage was a machine to support the *sarariman*, vital cog in the gears of business, to produce children, educate them, integrate them into a workforce. The state's dream machine. Marriage seldom satisfied the full needs of women, except as mothers, or the full needs of men, except as aliens or infants in their own homes. Exceptions doubtless abound. But the material is there, of tragedy, pathos, waste, art.

See Sawako Ariyoshi's *The Doctor's Wife*, Fumiko Enchi's *Masks*, Yuko Tsushima's *Woman Running in the Mountains*. Three generations of women novelists, three intricate visions of marriage and, in the last, of unwed motherhood. Or see the films of Juzo Itami—his best known in America is *Tampopo*, his most apposite here *Ageman*—who says, "Japan has not yet invented fatherhood as part of its culture. So where most societies have three main figures—father, mother, and child—Japan has only two, and men grow up to be children." It is what they call *mazakon* (mother complex).

I once teased a young friend who had studied in America (I would not have teased her otherwise), "Tell me the truth about all those rumors we hear, lesbianism, mother-son incest, various sexual accoutrements in homes with absent fathers or husbands." She shot back with a hint of smile: "No need. We have *furin* (adultery, immorality) now, as you do." There are also gigolos, specialized clubs, fantastic—I mean fantasy-filled—love hotels, all the compensations of lack. And a divorce rate still a quarter of America's.

Young women (nearly) know what they want and take their time before marriage. They have a *keep-kun* (friend on the side), an *ashi-kun* (to drive them around), *video-kun*, *mitsugu-kun* (gift-giver), *meshi-kun* (for dinners out), and hopefully a *honmei-kun* (real sweetheart). True, society as a whole still considers only married mothers *ichinin-mae* (adult, complete, respectable), and 88 percent of Japanese women marry by the age of thirty-five. True, magazines still counsel young women to be "maternal" to attract a future husband. True, women still lag behind men in salaries, prestige, power. True, pornography revels in mayhem to women, and ads often cultivate the pouty, vulnerable, almost abused, female look. And true, no woman has stepped in a sumo ring, not even to award a prize, in its 1,400-year history, though many are ardent, knowledgeable, front-row fans.

The scene offers no ideological comforts. But let us also remember, as Nobuko Sawanobori, president of a Tokyo marketing firm, says, "Men worked their butts off after the war. Women gathered their strength." She smiles (I imagine) without gloating.

NOISE

It comes from loudspeakers, mounted on cruising vans, blaring music and slogans. "Oh, those are rightist factions," an acquaintance explains, smiling, the Japanese equivalent of a shrug. It comes from piercing beepers, at the busy intersections of busy city streets. "That's for the blind, safely to cross." It comes from the sky, wafted by dirigibles. "They're advertising a new *pachinko* parlor." It comes from speakers hidden in trees—you can hear "Yankee Doodle" in the exquisite Rikugien Garden—from the megaphones of tour leaders, from construction jackhammers, from exercise songs in factories or pleasure songs in karaoke (empty orchestra) bars, from rock music roaring from mountain lookouts, from the peep, tinkle, ring, and squall of assorted household gadgets. "We are not particularly sensitive to noise," another acquaintance says, and smiles.

Well, the rightists have become more sophisticated: they now pipe more songs than slogans from their perambulating vans. The fact remains: modern Japan is noisy. What became of those acolytes of silence, votaries of the void, masters of evasion and implication, unembarrassed by long pauses in speech?

Japan is now urban—one-quarter of the total population lives in the Tokyo region—and cities are noisy. Japan is communal, if not quite Dionysiac, and sound unites while the eye distances. (Nietzsche knew that the ear has no earlids.) In any case, if privacy has its narrow place in Japan, togetherness has larger space. Then again, sound—loud sound—carries authority. The Japanese have nothing against authority.

Beyond that: tolerance for noise, tolerance for litter. I mean litter in unclaimed sites only: a deserted beach, an empty lot. Outlawed space. Donald Richie distinguishes two mental zones in Japan: first, my space or your space, all meticulously respected because clearly claimed; then the other kind of space, undefined, disprized, degraded—like some occupied territories in the Pacific war? In short, no sense of a public realm. Perhaps even no need of a public realm—parkland in Japan occupies an exiguous 2.2 square meters per capita compared to between thirty and fifty square meters in the Occident.

In Japanese politics, as in noise or litter, the res publica is absent as well—hence cyclopean corruption. It hardly exists even in karaoke bars, where each singer becomes his own Pavarotti or Sinatra, her own Kiri Te Kanawa or Aretha Franklin, belting out melodies to two or three friends in the audiences, perhaps only to the eclipsed star vocalist within. For the rest there, the song is comforting background noise.

But noise is also the other side of Japanese silence: the primal utterance of rocks in a Zen garden, the tacit understanding of mother and daughter, the reticence of fortitude.

ORDER (DISORDER) (See also Law)

Chaos theory, fuzzy logic, complexity. These newfangled sciences may someday shed light on social order (disorder) in Japan. I can't. It's all like Kafka's The Castle, which Einstein thought the human mind is insufficient to grasp.

I saw it first in the lovely asymmetry of things Japanese: earthen bowls, temple gardens, silk kimonos, lacquered boxes and screens, the bias of calligraphy, the shape of rice fields. Always the delight of surprise. I saw it next in the tug between set behavior—part ritual, part robotic—and the sudden break in pattern: excited scamper, comic turmoil, index fingers pointing every which way. I saw it later in domestic gadgetry, heaters with uncertain logic, computerized cars with a mind of their own. In all these, something beyond simple order or disorder, something ambiguous, like a Japanese sentence.

"We are not cold, logical people," the Japanese boast. "Not *rikutsuppoi*, reason freaks. Our sentences are richly ambiguous." Yes, of course, except in science, technology, commerce, the civil and military services, small things like that. But it is not finally a matter of heat or logic. The old, the mythic, core of society remains vital in Japan. So does the alogical spirit of Zen. Put another way, pragmatism prevails over principle. Where, then, is the contradiction, the paradox, the irony, the incongruity, of things? A Buddhist temple next to a power station? Of course.

That is not to say the Japanese are irrational, right-brained, left-handed creatures from outer space. (Schools, incidentally, firmly correct left-handed children.) History, institutions, luck, deprivations, give the Japanese character its texture. Despite their modular lives, their habit of obedience, their seeming naïveté, their fondness of repetition, the Japanese introduce something— call it subtlety, complexity, a touch of chaos—into existence.

I have watched some Japanese friends seat themselves around a large table in a restaurant, without place cards. I thought I had been transported to Egypt. Genial confusion, friendly pudder, ceremony in shards. Then something clicked. Suddenly, everyone was perfectly in place. We were back in Japan.

I have seen something similar with groups of inebriated businessmen on Ginza or Akasaka streets. One moment they gurgle and lurch, pretending to be hopelessly drunk. The next—under Sally's curious stare—they walk a straight line.

Is it a wonder that, like some others, I feel tempted by this knowing culture, with its invisible hand? Only tempted.

PRAGMATISM

"We are a pragmatic people"—you hear it all the time. What does it really mean?

"We are practical people, oriented toward action, unimpressed by abstract universals, the heirs of Zen, responsive to many gods, not just One." Yes, it could mean that. It could also mean, "We are averse to impersonal, logical principles, we do what's necessary; call us opportunists if you wish. You are the same, only more hypocritical." And it could trenchantly mean, as Robert J. Smith convincingly argues in *Japanese Society*, "We Japanese take the phenomenal world as absolute." What else can they be, then, but pragmatists?

But there is an ambiguity in the word itself. The *Oxford English Dictionary* gives these definitions for *pragmatism*: (1) relating to affairs of state; (2) busy, active, intrusive, meddling; (3) conceited, opinionated, dictatorial; (4) treating historical facts systematically; (5) practical, matter-of-fact, dealing with practice. That's language, a glorious, pragmatic welter of contradictions.

In common parlance, however, the term wavers between two senses, slips between a high and low register: Zen and rascality, William James and cynical expediency. Japanese politicians, negotiators, corporate managers, know how to play the entire register with finesse.

But James and Zen also understand one another. James: "There is no possible point of view from which the world can appear an absolutely single fact." Is this not the secret logic of the fifteen boulders in the Zen garden at Ryoanji, never visible all at the same time, from any single perspective? James again: Pragmatism "will count mystical experiences if they have practical consequences . . . will take a God who lives in the very dirt of private fact—if that should seem a likely place to find him." What Zen patriarch would deny it? And again James: "What is mind? No matter. What is matter? Never mind." To the Japanese, this is banal.

Still, there are differences. Pragmatism means pluralism for James, Charles Sanders Peirce, Richard Rorty. Not for the Japanese. Pragmatism offers James "manners various and flexible"; it "unstiffens." But it stiffens Japanese conformity, offers no challenge to their exclusiveness or hunger for purity. In Japan, pragmatism and purity, pragmatism of the blood, cohesion, the old imperative of survival. Pragmatism in every respect, and to any limit, to preserve what Lafcadio Hearn called the Race Ghost.

Is that pragmatism prescient or retrograde? I think not the former: I have placed my bet on an uncircumscribed world. "There is no outside, no enclosing wall, no circumference to us," said Emerson, the American pragmatist, in his great, sad essay, "Experience." Just so.

QUIRKS

No nation is without its eccentrics, no culture without quirks. The Japanese, though, know how to smooth human surfaces. This does not mean they eliminate individuality completely. As Edwin O. Reischauer reminds us, many Japanese still see themselves "as fiercely individualistic, high-principled, self-disciplined and aesthetically sensitive modern-day Musashis"—referring to the intractable, peerless seventeenth-century swordsman.

Still, I encountered few Japanese so quirky or anomalous as to seem grotesque. Yes, of course, there are Kabuki masks, ukiyo-e prints, *manga* strips, Buddhist warrior statues grimacing fearfully at us. But unlike the characters of Sherwood Anderson and William Faulkner, Flannery O'Connor and Carson McCullers, Japanese literature rarely portrays the deeper isolation, psychic violence, of the human grotesque. No metaphysical blights like Ahab's, immemorial guilts like the Pyncheons. Not the monstrous frolics, insatiable expectations, of the American self.

Exception: certain Japanese individuals, living abroad. Something happens to particular exiles, when their myths unravel, their inhibitions shred. A kind of anarchy or frenzy takes over. Their reactions become a little crazed, like fanatics of the Red Army Faction or the Kwantung Army in Manchuria.

I know someone like that. He has long lived in America, too long to be called, by the Japanese, Japanese. Hunched shoulders, cratered face, a laugh laced with anger and contumely. In him, adaptation has gone somehow haywire: the best of two cultures has vanished, the worst of both remains. His character seems full of unexpected cracks, through which paranoia twists. He will countenance no criticism of Japan—the accusation of racism rushes easily to his lips—which he unstintingly derides. Thus must he continually defend what he continually attacks. The effort has morally deformed him, as if tattooed beneath the skin.

Quirks. Of course you can find them in Japan. For instance, in *irezumi*, tattooing. More than any people, more than the Maoris even, the Japanese have developed and sustained tattooing into an art. Originally the mark of outcasts—criminals, *burakumin*, untouchables, renegades—it became later the defiant badge of roughs, firemen in the Edo Period, *yakuzas* to this day. Toughs and laborers of every kind, from construction workers to sushi makers. Still, if you ask some Japanese, they will answer, "Oh, that was in the old days. No tattooing now." (Mischievously, I refer them to the gorgeously illustrated volume of Donald Richie and Ian Buruma, *The Japanese Tattoo.*)

But I understand the denial. Tattoo, once a sign of ostracism, remains socially disreputable, déclassé, at best an oddity on the margins of the beautiful and the weird. Banned in the Meiji Period for fear of international ridicule, it was permitted again only—savor the irony—with the occupation of postwar Japan. Nowadays, some trendy youngsters, affecting the proletariat, may flaunt tattoos.

Put simply, too simply, in a culture of surfaces, of appearances, quirks tend to surface—they never have the chance to sink very deeply.

RIVALRY

Rivalry? In a cooperative, cohesive society? Indeed. "Competition is what we have instead of creativity," an office manager once confided to me. "For us, it serves the same purpose." And it serves well since rivalry operates within a framework of conformity, in tension with *wa*, harmony.

How else could it be in a group-minded society? Everyone watching, watching especially peers. A temporal hierarchy: he was one year ahead of me in school, she was two years behind, we are of the same class and age. Watching, appraising, competing. Who's stumbled? Who's ahead? And by how many millimeters?

When word went out in the Ministry of Foreign Affairs to work fewer hours in order to improve Japan's workaholic image, ambitious men sneaked into the ministry at night through the back door. "It's not only the work ethic," a diplomat told me. "You just can't afford to fall behind others." That man now holds the highest ambassadorial rank.

All this makes for a certain drive, perfectionism, a substitute for originality. Without rocking the boat. Without "selfishness." This rivalry, after all, is not really personal. It is in the system, for the system. Even in the sleazy Kabuki-cho district, in Tokyo, where the huge, lurid signs of bars, massage parlors, and porno shops try to outscream one another in the same alley.

The women, of course, compete less. They are sisterly, seem sisterly, without benefit of ideology. It is their historical position, now changing as they begin to compete with one another as well as with men. Still, I have not seen an elegant woman cast at another that look, sharper than splintered glass, common in Beverly Hills or Dallas.

Perhaps the ethos of rivalry is due to the genius of Japan, a mimetic, reactive genius, at least traditionally, rarely initiative, even as an economic superpower, always prudent—what will others say, what will they do? Or perhaps, as I have suggested, rivalry is the gristle of cohesion, the spine of loyalty. In any case, it is sustained since infancy by the kyoiku mama (education mama). Sustained by the school examination system. Sustained by the practice of hiring, promotion. And yet few fall by the wayside. They may not arrive at the top. They may get the madogiwa-zoku (the window seat), as the incompetent do, to gaze out their lives till retirement. But if they play the game, rivalry included, they will be cared for.

Rivalry, conformity, mimesis. The quick glance, stolen over the shoulder, out of the corner of the eye. It is particularly quick, guarded, when one Japanese espies another at some tony place abroad, say the Connaught in London, Castel in Paris, the opera at Bayreuth.

SWORDS

They surpass the finest Toledo or Solingen steel. Slice through flesh and bone as easily as through armor, silk, hair. They have geometric, no, mystic brilliance, a pure line, the curvature of eternity. In them, sheer form and sheer function are wedded beyond death. They flash out of their scabbards only to kill. Best of all, the sword that never has to leave its sheath. You polish a sword as a soul is polished.

Musashi could fashion a sword from a wooden oar and win his duel on the island of Funashima. That is because the Way of the Sword was a complete way: physical, intellectual, above all spiritual, a fusion of man and nature. But the old master swordsmiths—Masatsune, Tomonari, Mitsuyo, Norimune—worked in steel, smelted the ore, forged the iron, folded the glowing blade countless times upon itself, tempered it in hissing water, honed it till it acquired a supernal sheen. Earth, Fire, Water, Air: the ageless, magic combat of the elements with one another—and with Art. Add also the fifth element: the void.

Some say the history of the sword and the history of Japan are one. That may be nostalgia. Certainly the technology of steel informs Japanese politics, Japanese culture. Certainly, swords, since Prince Shotoku, passed from one generation to another. Mounted or bare, they spoke of pride, achievement, devotion, skill. Useless in their gorgeous, lacquered scabbards, they signified across time. The emperor's sacred emblems: Mirror, Jewel, Sword.

But what does it all mean for postmodern Japan? All those swords with illustrious names, glinting in their glass cases?

I acknowledge the beauty, the purity, the terror of a sword in its intimacy with death. Its real sheath is human flesh, its real scabbard, our mortality. And I understand Nobuie when he engraves a sword guard: "Oh, how happy I am. No one thinks of me as human and I think of no one as human." The freedom of that "inhumanity"—the legendary swordsmen understood it.

But what does it all mean to office ladies, salarymen? The clue may be in myself. What business had I to frequent such places as the Japanese Sword Museum at Sangubashi? It was not only a "man's thing." Sally found these steely emblems breathtaking. She found them eloquent in history, not inhuman but all too human, sculptures—the sveltest Brancusi—steeped in anger, ambition, pain. I, too, found in them something penetrating the hype and noise of a consumer, a media society. Was that nostalgia?

If so, it was, for the Japanese at least, nostalgia of a special kind. One says to me, "Our swords were not meant, like yours, to hew and hack other swords. They flashed only once through the air to kill." I think: here is the ruthless economy of Japan, in one aesthetic gesture. But another says, "We are tired of the samurai ethic. It does not represent Japan. Beside the small samurai class, we had peasants, artisans, merchants. And for 250 years under the Tokugawas, the samurai had nothing to do."

Still, the swords glisten on their stands, in lucent cases, dreaming hard dreams of yore. Dreams of days before guns displaced them (1543), before the Emperor Meiji prohibited his subjects to carry them (1876). Yes, swords had a purity I did not find in America or modern Egypt, only in certain Pharaonic forms, say Horus on the wing. But is not that very purity a shadow of things past, which no longing or remembrance can return?

TRAVEL

It would have to be domestic. Travel within Japan, not this pointless "traipsing" (Kawabata) all over the world. After all, the vast majority of Japanese still hold no passports.

Once, Japan had a navy, pirates, overseas traders, explorers. Perhaps not like Ibn Batuta, Columbus, Magellan, or Drake, but enterprising, roving enough. For instance, in the ninth century, Prince Takuoka—see Tatsuhiko Shibusawa's *Sea Travels of Prince Takuoka*. Then the third Tokugawa shogun decreed that the nation should be preserved forever in amber.

After that, only pilgrims, priests, ronin (literally, wave men, masterless samurai), artists, actors, mendicants moved about. Inside Japan. Sometimes they were heroes, more often wretches, cut off from village and home. Who would not be wretched, braving brigands, floods, hunger, disease, the wrath of warlords, the cold, pitiless wind from the mountains? To mitigate the miseries, an inspired wanderer, perhaps a series of poet-priests, thus formulated the rules of the road, according to Oliver Statler in *Japanese Inn*:

Be prepared to die at any time. Don't think of tomorrow: tomorrow will take care of itself. Life is vanity.

Put away carnal desires, as well as hope for honors and luxuries.

Observe the five commandments of Buddhism, which forbid killing, stealing, fornication, drinking, and idle talk. (However, there can be exceptions for drink and a little idle talk.)

Give everything down to the skin if you meet with highwaymen. Be ready to give up your life if they want to kill you, and never fight back.

Don't higgle over ferry and inn charges, and tip as one should.

Give alms to beggars and medicine to the sick when you meet them on the way.

Never refuse a request for calligraphy, but never offer it

unless requested. Plagiarism is taboo.

Never ride a horse or kago, except in places where it is very difficult to go by foot.

And when you feel inclined to break these rules, stop your journey and go home.

But difficulties do not stymy the Japanese. Lafcadio Hearn noted a century ago, "The man of the people in America cannot compare, as a traveler, with the man of the people in Japan. . . . [The Japanese] are the greatest travelers because, even in a land composed mainly of mountain chains, they recognize no obstacles to travel."

Travel now engrosses 76 percent of the Japanese. Travel in families, travel in groups. Travel as tourists or pilgrims. Travel to get away, indulge fantasies of freedom—"a traveler has no shame," the saying goes. Travel to commune with one another, do something glamorous that others do. I doubt that many, in this urban nation, however Shinto in creed, now travel to commune with Nature. Gone are the visions of Hiroshige along the old Tokaido Road.

I once took an overnight ferry from Owarai, on Honshu, to Tomakomai, on Hokkaido. Twenty hours. The weather gradually cleared, the low sky turned from lead to high cobalt blue, with scudding white clouds. Sally and I walked the decks, scanned the shore with binoculars, peered under tarpaulins, climbed up and down hidden stairs, counted the ships to port and starboard, pounded the decks some more. The Japanese stayed below, except to snap a group picture against the seascape. Sally said, "Imagine a British ferry. They'd all be outside lounging in deck chairs or taking brisk turns." "Or leaning on the rails, gazing at the horizon," I replied.

For most Japanese, reality is not *there*, it is *here*, where they all are. No wanderlust, no great yearning for the exotic. But you can collect legitimate travel experiences. At the Furano Prince, a resort hotel in central Hokkaido, there is a lobby desk with eight rubber stamps on a rotating stand. You can choose one of them to stamp your Prince Hotel Travel Passport. A souvenir. You don't need really to apply for a passport, go abroad.

I look at the handsome toy seals—one or two a bit Disneyish—and wonder, well, what's wrong with it? The pleasures are innocent, even if the profits go to the Prince Corporation. No, I think, Reality is not always Here, it's also There, where the differences are. Then I say to myself, oh, relax, it's just a game children play at a resort.

URBANISM (See *also* Fax)

The cities are not beautiful, except sometimes where they meet the sea: Yokohama, Hiroshima, Fukuoka, also called Hakata. How could they be? Most were razed during the war. Still, ugly or beautiful, they are what most Japanese inhabit. Inhabit while treasuring a primal memory or illusion of some village remote in childhood.

Japan: urban bodies, rural souls. Shinto gods in an asphalt and concrete wilderness, gnarled, listing utility poles, dreary hutches, steel crash guards instead of sidewalks. An affluent, bustling wilderness, though. Already, in the eighteenth century, Edo was more populous than any European capital.

And why say "wilderness"? Yes, vast urban tracts spread remorselessly across the landscape, gray, modular, jerry-built structures, displacing the fabled integrity of the old, wooden Japanese houses. A kind of ashen, manmade lava, climbing slowly—what sacrilege—toward the peak of Fuji? Unthinkable. The slopes and base of the mountain have mercifully become a national park;

the effluence has taken to the air, industrial smog shrouding the matchless peak on most days.

Yes, urban sprawl; yes, towering blight, which the Japanese hardly notice. But as Italo Calvino says in *Invisible Cities*, one may "discern, through the walls and towers destined to crumble, the tracery of a pattern so subtle it could escape the termites' gnawing." The interior pattern of Japanese cities is, as in all great cities, noetic, the sculpture of human vitality, semiosis unlimited. But sculpture or semiosis with a Nippon twist. Call it coded anarchy.

Consider the implausible: greater Tokyo itself, rebuilt after innumerable fires, earthquakes, bombings, now some twenty-five, perhaps already thirty million inhabitants in an area of 2,500 square miles. Pollution, congestion, toxic belts, slapdash suburbs, noodling streets. But what abundance of the human. What variety, cleanliness, efficiency in services. And nearly crime free! You say, a megamachine? Well, the Japanese do not feel they are worthless cogs in a machine. As Peter Popham puts it rather enthusiastically in *Tokyo: The City at the End of the World*: "In the West the realization that one is a cog in a machine is a source of shame, a reason for rebellion. In Tokyo, when you realize what a damn-near flawless and unprecedentedly magnificent machine you are a perfect cog in, it is, on the contrary, a matter of blissful contemplation."

Japanese cities resemble other cities only to the degree that Japanese culture emulates other cultures: the differences are also real. Where but in Tokyo would space capsules inspire an architect, Kisho Kurokawa, to build apartments that are replaceable containers, as in the Nakagin Capsule Building? Or a house, like Takamitsu Azuma's, rise four floors on a plot of only 215 square feet, a nearly triangular tower, just a miraculous staircase really, still serving as a comfortable family home? Or a narrow, zebra-

striped, eight-story, postmodern structure—Minoru Takeyama's Ichibankan in East Shinjuku—house forty-nine tiny bars? Or air-conditioned boxes, enlarged coffins really, supplied with TV, radio, and reading lights, function as hotel rooms? Or bed-towns crawl along private railroad lines emanating from, and owned by, giant *depatos* like Seibu or Odakyu? Or a ceremonial rice paddy flourish within the Imperial Palace grounds, invisible to all but a few citizens, at the very center of the city? Or love hotels, perhaps the ultimate (non) architecture of desire, pop up in the most unlikely nooks of the urbanscape?

Japanese cities, Japanese architects: surely the most innovative and outré in the world. The great names roll off the tongue: Tadao Ando, Arata Isozaki, Kenzo Tange, Fumihiko Maki, joined by others I have mentioned, and others more radical still, like Makoto Sei Watanabe or Ryoji Suzuki. Chaotic and unsightly as they may be, Japanese cities have liberated a space for architectural genius, a carnival of designs—and of messages from the global village. No integration expected in these sculptures of human energy. Time made visible, as the Japanese travel from one era to another in their gnostic cities.

VERACITY

Poor Townsend Harris, the first consul general of the United States, of any foreign nation, in Japan. Stubborn, irascible, dyspeptic, lonely. Oh, he got at last his trade treaty, got it at long last. But he complained and complained about Japanese veracity.

After one incident of prevarication—out of how many in his three years at Shimoda?—he exploded in his diary: "It is all of a piece with their falsehood and duplicity. I do not think that any Japanese ever tells the truth, if it can possibly be avoided." This is the same man who, on first arriving in Japan in 1856, wrote: "We were all much pleased with the appearance and

manners of the Japanese. I repeat, they are superior to any people east of the Cape of Good Hope." And this is the same man who, five years later, would again write: "I would sooner see all the Treaties with this country torn up, and Japan return to its old state of isolation, than witness the horrors of war inflicted on this peaceful people and happy land."

I know just what Harris means in all three statements. Veracity is but one focus of a stranger's mixed admiration and exasperation in Japan. I have never known a people more truthful in daily life—they rarely lie, as others do, out of cowardice or personal gain. But I have never known a people so subtle in avoiding the truth where cultural values sanction the evasion—saving face, avoiding confrontation, serving group interests.

Truth, veracity, verism, verisimilitude. The Japanese do not imitate reality; they construct, abstract, ritualize it. Yes, yes, they are adept imitators, copycats if you wish. But that's in a different realm, with foreign things and fashions. Their native tradition, in all the arts—realists like Shoyo Tsubouchi notwithstanding—refuses mimesis. Their "truth"? Not one of correspondence but of intuition, formal coherence, that is, poesis. A truth of naturalness, say of the first tea master, Rikyu, who scattered a few autumn leaves on the garden path to his teahouse, which his son had mistakenly swept too clean.

What, then, can veracity mean to a people who disdain ethical or artistic realism? No and Kabuki differ from social life only in degree. Mythic ethos, formal aesthetic, and ritual allegiance still suffuse daily existence.

Veracity? Vulgar verism? In what context? To what end?

WAR CRIMES

Atrocities. What war, what nation, is exempt from them? What person does not feel or pretend revulsion?

I have never visited Japan without thinking: those horrors. I have seldom found in Japan, as I have often found in Germany, someone with whom I could speak candidly about war crimes. National denial, personal denial—they coincide under the sign of the rising sun.

Perhaps there is nothing more to say. Perhaps everything. The books continue—*The Other Nüremberg, Soldiers of the Sun, In the Realm of a Dying Emperor, Japan at War: An Oral History*—the debates on textbooks persist, the forms of self-censorship remain. Shall we apologize to Asians? Can cabinet ministers worship at the Yasukuni War Shrine? Will the emperor visit China?

True, we dropped the bomb. Yes, B-29s left Japanese cities in rubble and flames. And we interned a hundred thousand nisei, sansei, to our everlasting shame. But there was also Pearl Harbor, Bataan, all those coral islands—Tarawa, Iwo Jima, Saipan, Peleliu, Okinawa—bloody red, bloodiest of all the prospect of invading the Japanese archipelago. (When Japan surrendered, Korea celebrated August 15 as Return of Light Day.) The hopeless calculus of guilt, of endless retribution.

I do not calculate when I am in Japan. I say to myself, "You chose America." What kind of world would it have been, with Hitler, Tojo, Mussolini at the top? We know what kind of world. And so I go back to vex the question: Why did the Japanese do it?

"We are a pragmatic, not a reflective, people," some say. "We revere strength, purity, endurance, pride, the samurai's ethic. Cruelty is only the dark side of our idealism," others add. "We feel no shame, no obligation, toward outsiders," still others admit. And more defiantly: "They surrendered. How can we respect them—you call them 'prisoners of war'?" Then the layered cultural cringe: "Remember, for a hundred years, we only wanted one thing, to surpass the West."

The historical, the human mystery remains, the calculus loses track of itself. The Japanese have been taught how much they suffered, never how much suffering they have inflicted. Three million lost Japanese lives, yes, but also fifteen million Chinese lives alone.

Not all Japanese have taken the vow of silence, though. Writers, intellectuals, a few professors, the mayor of Nagasaki—these speak up. Shusaku Endo speaks up in his novel, *The Sea and Poison*, based on a wartime "incident," the vivisection of some American flyers in Kyushu. Still, what can a novel do? What difference can it finally make?

The novel perdures. We read it, reread it, remember its characters speak; we read and remember in many languages. For instance,

—The postwar narrator: "I thought of the training regiment to which I had been assigned. In the dimly lit orderly rooms had sat any number of shrewd-faced men like the gas station owner. While they were berating us recruits, their cruel, narrow eyes would glitter with unmistakable pleasure."

—The gas station attendant: "But we had our fun in China too. Did whatever we wanted with the women. Any bastard that made any complaints we tied to a tree and used for target practice."

—A Japanese nurse in Manchuria: "Ueda told me that it was the way those Manchurians were. You had to knock them around. . . . And, sure enough, I soon got in the habit of hitting [the maid], for no reasons at all."

—Toda, a doctor who helped perform the vivisections: "To put it quite bluntly, I am able to remain quite undisturbed in the face of someone else's terrible suffering and death."

—On the officers watching the experiment: "Actually, all of them had faces flushed with blood and covered with sweat—the sort of look which follows upon sexual consummation."

—Toda, again, to Suguro, who refuses at the last moment to participate in the murder: "What is it that gets you? . . . Killing that prisoner? Thanks to him, we'll now be better at curing thousands of TB patients. . . . Answer for it? To society? If it's only to society, it's nothing much to get worked up about. . . . You and I happened to be here in this particular hospital in this particular era, and so we took part in a vivisection performed on a prisoner. If those people who are going to judge us had been put in the same situation, would they have done anything different?"

Some would have. That's Endo's point, a Christian's. And it becomes the reader's.

I know the contingency of terror, anywhere, any time, in my own city, Jeffrey Dahmer's. But no more than Endo—who humanizes, particularizes, all his characters—no more than him can I believe that only societies have eyes. For then, everything is permitted, permitted out of sight, in the dark.

XENOPHOBIA

A Clash lyric reminds the "Bamboo Kid" that blood feeds on rice, not "Coca-Cola."

Enough, enough said on the subject. Or is it ever enough? After all, Japan has only opened its doors under duress, inch by excruciating inch, and still the door seems shut. You have to read the minute, painful details—in Oliver Statler's *Shimoda Story*—to believe that infinite reluctance, avoidance. Saying all the while, politely, "Please understand."

Xenophobia: the other face of loyalty. Once, in Nagasaki, grim irony, I lectured to the *Nichibei-kai* (Japanese-American society). The topic was travel as metaphor of the new internationalism. At the end of the talk, a trim, middle-aged lady stood up after the requisite, seemingly interminable silence that must follow every lecture in Japan. She said in a level voice, "Thank you very much for your lecture. All this travel and internationalism are very interesting. But you know, we are first of all Japanese, and we must remember that." I replied, "Of course. But what comes second?" I believe that for her nothing did. Loyalty ended at the gray-and-black-sand beaches of the Japanese archipelago.

Foreigners have their stories of aversion, say, about the Japanese moving away from them on the subway. Discreetly, of course, as if to give the gaijin more space. But it never happened to us.

Oh, yes, once. On the Odakyu Line, hurtling toward Shinjuku. The man looked as if he had come from central casting: a thick laborer, about four feet six, with gap teeth, bleary eyes, battered face, clad in working knickers and a rumpled cap. When he saw, no, felt us standing next to him in the crowded car, an ancient intelligence lit his eyes. He smiled broadly to himself, as if recalling an old joke. And he moved quietly to the next car. I remembered then reading in Statler about the townsfolk who wanted to burn a bench on which foreign sailors had sat, back in the last days of the last shogun. And I, too, smiled.

But it happened only once. And who knows what ran through the man's mind?

Still, indubitably, many Japanese, especially in small towns and rural areas, dislike foreigners. Their feeling can become intense. And it can turn inward, a xenophobia within, creating various outcasts, like the burakumin, who sometimes blacken their faces to heighten their outcast fate.

Once, in the shadow of the White House, I exchanged some pleasantries with a black panhandler. A Japanese couple, old friends, happened to be visiting with us in the scandalous capital. The wife whispered to Sally in polite shock, "Ihab talks to beggars?" I thought then of a Mongoloid child I once saw playing alone in a Nagoya park, wholly invisible to every passer by. Was this invisibility politeness? Or an absolute rejection of difference? (Deformity in Japan is shameful; hence, in part, the power of Kenzaburo Oe's fictions, inspired by his retarded son.)

The power to ignore, to exclude, to shut out completely. The Japanese possess it instinctively, implacably. A truly magical, apotropaic power. Deny cancer—doctors will rarely tell you, anyway. Deny social failures—let them sleep in cemeteries for criminals or ride with motorcycle gangs passing through villages in the night. Sometimes I think that all Japan wants to be immaculate, like the sacred island of Miyajima, where none is allowed to give birth or die.

How can this magical temper persist in the twentieth, almost the twenty-first, century? Japanese intellectuals wonder too. They do more. Some champion pariahs, as Kenji Nakagami did in his novel, *Misaki*, which won the Akutagawa Prize in 1976. Others decry the stubborn seclusion of Japan, as did Kanji Nishio in *A Strategy of National Isolation*. "I feel very strongly the isolation of Japan battling the West alone," Nishio says in a panel discussion. "We have neither Asia nor the West to turn to. We are truly a lonely nation." But is not the seed of xenophobia in this self-fulfilling plaint, which even intellectuals continue to plant?

The other face of xenophobia: Yamatoism (a term coined by the sociologist, William Wetherall), the original race, Yamato min-*zoku*, the unique Japanese spirit, the Race Ghost. These ideas have advocates in high places. Advocates of a "wet climate" and the "monoracial state" (former Prime Minister Yasuhiro Nakasone), of the unique receptivity of the Japanese brain to certain sounds (Dr. Tadanobu Tsunoda), of a variety of mystic nationalisms (Takeshi Umehara, Shintaro Ishihara).

Of course, all these are not the same. Rightists, Yamatoists, *yakuzas* come in a great many shades. Still, their rhetoric includes words like soil, soul, blood, race—I almost added *Heimat*. Even professors of foreign languages become Yamatoists, the noisiest kind; they "look through a whiskey glass," as Ian Buruma quips in *God's Dust*, "and hope to find pure blood." For the more the Japanese borrow or imitate, the more they seem to protest their purity and uniqueness.

I honor the Japanese in their immense task of self-fashioning, self-creation, in the shadow of Western modernity. I attempted a personal version of that task when I left Egypt. But I worry, just a little, about that Bamboo Kid in the Clash lyric. And I wonder about those signs on baggage carts at Narita Airport: "Import. It keeps the world together." Really? Suddenly I realize: those signs in English address mainly gaijin.

YES?

Yes, yes, it's been often said about the Japanese: don't take yes for an answer. They decline confrontations, they are accomplices of silence. But the Japanese do say yes and say it with various shades and colors of agreement. They say "Hai" with alacrity, not only in obedience—the German *Jawohl, Herr Kapitan*—but also in respect for the interlocutor, in awareness of sociability. For despite all its absences, Japanese culture can be affirmative.

Affirmative but not metaphysical. The Japanese *yes* is not ontological, the rock of Being, the great cry "I AM!" The Japanese *yes* is more relational, often closer to *so desu* (yes, I see; oh, I see), a response to a human event or presence. It can therefore shift subtly to neutral acknowledgment or phatic sound.

So how can you tell: is it yes, no, perhaps? The Japanese have a saying, "He's so stupid, he must be told in words." Which really means: context is all, either you are attuned to it or not.

That is why foreigners have trouble with the Japanese *yes*, as they do with so much else besides.

But context is not really all. Watch the body talk, watch the eyes, as the great swordsmen did. The Japanese may use a tensing of shoulders, a narrowing of pupils, to contradict you. (Gestures are expressive and gendered: men point aggressively with the index finger, women wave toward the object with a cupped hand.) Facial expressions, grimaces, are visible beneath the mask.

I have said Japanese culture is affirmative. It is also inertial. Because it is still profoundly conservative, ruled by ancestors from the grave, ruled by the past. This means that Japan also says "No" continually, says it with a roar on the other side of its deference. Says No to Time, No to Change, while accepting the impermanence of all worldly things. Paradoxes again.

In this sense, the Japan That Can Say Yes is more worthy than Shintaro Ishihara's *The Japan That Can Say No*, with its fatuous invocations of the superior "Japanese blood," its primitive reversions behind geopolitical chatter and threats of World War III. That deeper *hai*, how much more liberating, enabling.

ZEN

DONALD RICHIE

He came, he saw, he stayed, has stayed for almost half a century now. He found in Japan his freedom, equivocal freedom.

We first met under allegorical—or was it preternatural?—conditions at the International House of Tokyo in 1989. I was giving a talk then on "The Burden of Mutual Perception" between Japan and the United States. How end such a talk, without sentimentality or recrimination? I found my parable in Donald Richie's book, *Different People,* a gallery of beguiling verbal etchings.

The story is this. While still a member of the occupation forces, Richie met Yasunari Kawabata. Richie could not speak Japanese then, Kawabata could not speak English, and their interpreters defected at the last moment. Nonetheless, the two men climbed together the Asakusa Tower, "with everything to say to each other and no way to say it." Richie writes: "On that cold day in 1947 Asakusa was a burned-out plain along the river with only a few buildings, our tower among them, still standing. There was no Asakusa Kannon Temple: it had been destroyed and was only later reconstructed." After an hour, the two men, chilled by the January air, repaired to a coffee shop, and warming themselves by a hibachi, drank bitter Black Arabian. They also had their "literary conversation": "I said: Gide. He looked thoughtful, nodded, then said: Mann. I thought, then said *Tonio Kröger,* at which he broke into a smile and said: *Der Zauberberg.* We thus talked about Flaubert, Poe, Zweig. I drew a blank on Proust because he had not yet been translated into Japanese. He received nothing for Colette because I did not yet know this great writer." And so it went between them, a happy conversation, even if neither mentioned *Moby Dick, Leaves of Grass,* or *Huckleberry Finn.* Richie then concludes, "What struck me then and strikes me now about this literary non-encounter is not how much we couldn't say, but how much we managed to communicate.... When I now read a Kawabata novel and observe a person silent but aware, knowing an emotion but not partaking of it, I see Kawabata on that cold January afternoon."

I ended my talk by remarking,

"Different People": that is indeed what Americans and Japanese are, and their cultures, however hybrid now, are different cultures. But Richie and Kawabata could "translate" not only because they reached to one another in empathy, but also because they cared terribly, cared passionately and intelligently, about something else: Literature. Or was it really something larger even than literature, which they could both enter, carrying lightly their burden of mutual perception, shedding their differences? True, there is the rest of us, most of us, who in a crisis remain locked in our ideologies or tribes.

I had first encountered Richie between the covers of a book, *Different People;* I met him next in person, quoting him at the International House, where he materialized in the audience, with the hint of a quizzical smile as he heard himself quoted. We have met many times since, in Tokyo, in Milwaukee. A solid, square-faced man—at rest, he seems granite—with a lightning intelligence that can divine what you mean to say as you plod on. A man with sapient, sometimes satirical eyes that quietly penetrate people, places, the arbitrariness of existence.

Richie first came to Japan in 1947, as a civilian member of the Allied occupation. Interludes in New York—as film curator of the Museum of Modern Art—and in the Midwest, as Toyota Professor at the University of Michigan. But it has been Japan, really, ever since. More than forty books: countless essays, poems, *Kyogen*, novels, films, reviews. Prizes, it seems, on every continent except Antarctica. A blitz typist, accomplished pianist, a connoisseur of eels, islands, tattoos. Above all, perhaps, of Japanese cinema: Kurosawa, Ozu, Mizoguchi, Imamura, Oshima, Itami. *Time* calls him the doyen of art critics in Japan, and *Time* does not know the half of it. You can panic reading his vita.

But what is he doing in Japan? Following his nature, you might say, his vocations and avocations. It is like living on a mountain ridge, he teases in an interview: one valley is your country, and "you can see it as it truly is," and in the other you can "see wonderful Japan, [wonderful] simply because you're never allowed to go there.... You can compare, and comparison is freedom."

For Richie, freedom leads through archipelagos of choice toward self-knowledge. That is what his marvelous book, *The Inland Sea*, is about: not only talismans of the Japanese past, hidden on remote islands that shimmer between sea and sky, but also that interior journey we all undertake on the way to death. Meantime, there are the islands: "One could stay here a year or a day and never know the difference.

These islands are like the great undersea palaces visited by Urashima Taro, the fairy-tale hero who finally returned to discover that he had spent not a week but a lifetime. He found himself old and his children's children grown." If Richie ends his travel memoir by saying, "I don't care if I never go home," that is because he feels already there.

But Richie's other home, worldly and fugacious, is Tokyo, is modern Japan itself, a museum with crumbling walls. About that country, he has written—in A Lateral View, for instance—with unwavering acumen and concinnity. The terse style never flinches; we wither with it into perception. Illusion and claptrap fall away.

Self-exiled in Japan for as long as I have been in America, Donald Richie understands the deep cunning of cultural and psychic exchanges. But I may belong finally to America more than he was permitted to belong to Japan.

PART VI

ENVOY

BETWEEN THE EAGLE
AND THE SUN?

Late in his life, the poet William Butler Yeats kept a Japanese sword on his desk:

> Two heavy trestles, and a board
> Where Sato's gift, a changeless sword,
> By pen and paper lies,
> That it may moralise
> My days out of their aimlessness. . . .
> Chaucer had not drawn breath
> When it was forged.

The sword did not help Ireland or Japan. But it may have inspired Yeats. I understand his gesture.

Born in Egypt to fustian and a tumult of impotent passions, I too may have sought in Japan an insubstantial sword to "moralise my days." But quests, I have already said, lie within. Why then, even as I write this envoy, do I plot to return to Japan? I know now what I will not find there.

I will not find the "open society," the "happy country." State and society blur in Japan; authority has no boundaries. Where may citizens find their rights? Even when Japan borrowed from T'ang China (618–907), borrowed during the tenth and eleventh centuries, poets like Li Po and Tu Fu were shunned in favor of the milder Po Chüi because they criticized authority, because they subverted. "While over the centuries political integration increased and a national culture evolved," Karel van Wolferen notes, "there was no parallel development of the idea of belonging to a state." Japan remains an oxymoron: a feudal, albeit supertechnological, non-Western society, patterned superficially on modern Occidental nation states.

I will not find "criticism" there either, except as one work of art may criticize another and appearances qualify or displace other appearances. How else could it be? The most famous "photograph" of the Emperor Meiji is a version of an idealized painting, and a person's *hanko* (seal), easy to forge, is more authentic than his or her signature. So-called leftist critiques—oh, yes, Marxism was once de rigeur in certain circles, the very badge of intelligence: you were Marxist or you were Stupid—cultivated by chic, cranky ideologues wearing black turtleneck sweaters and a deep scowl, barely visible behind cigarette smoke—so-called leftist critiques became exercises in truculent illusions and high IQ follies. Hence the atrophy of the Japanese Socialist Party.

Nor will I find in Japan enhancement of my empathy for "difference" or knowledge of the world, except, ironically, knowledge of America. For I have come to believe that Japan will never act but on the narrowest construction of its self-interest: never, never, never, never, never. What knowledge, then, of America, could Japan yield? Insight, I think, into the intricacies of memory. Generous and well-meaning as conquerors, Americans have become complicit in postwar anti-Americanism. It is really the lesson of all conquests, all good intentions: they have a knack for reversing, perverting themselves. Living in Japan, I began to see America with some clarity, I mean see its shadows, too: how magnanimity breeds resentment and bigotry dances to a liberal tune.

And of course I could not expect to find in Japan enrichment of my individuality, realize there the ego's amplitude. "In the long centuries between Lady Murasaki's day and the late nineteenth century, there is seldom a voice that speaks to us with a truly personal note," remarks Donald Keene. As in literature, even more in life, the personal voice seems superfluous; each individual act must pass muster with the group. This phenomenon is nowhere more egregious than when a foreigner dates a Japanese girl—who then becomes, in the eyes of many compatriots, a whore.

The gifts of Japan are of another kind: not an open but a loyal, ceremonious society; not critical intelligence, but human intuition, artistic tact; not citizenship in the world but harmony on an island; not the discrete but the collective, sometimes cosmic, self. And just as certain regions—Kyushu, Shikoku, Chiba, Ibaraki—felt the long, cold hand of the Tokugawa shogunate more lightly than others, so do many regions of Japanese culture nearly escape the deadening uniformity of the country as a whole.

With half of my mind, I have learned in Japan to wink at *tatemae* (pretence, excuse), at the pervasive *kata* (form, formula) for each and every thing, at enforced courtesy, *yasashii* shading into *uetto* (wet)—*pace* Margaret Thatcher. Wink also at the cramped pessimism of the *Hojoki* (1212), Buddhist renunciation, aesthetic sacrifice, Tanizaki's reign of shadows—as well as crowds, kitsch, compulsive gift-giving, so much else besides.

With the other half, I have learned to value restraint, which Chikamatsu thought, in his renowned essay on the puppet theater, to inspire the highest pathos. Learned to appreciate lessness, though tempted myself by extravagance. Learned also to see "rust," how the Japanese wash it out with *shuyo* (self-discipline) or *seishinshugi* (spirit over matter). And learned to honor, most remarkable of all, a complex Japanese virtue, compounded of courage, loyalty, fortitude, and a kind of impersonal compassion, abyssal calm—a virtue we are as likely to encounter in *A Book of Five Rings* (1645) as on an NHK-TV program.

With both parts of my mind, though, I have tried to recall particular people in their full quiddity, hoping to find in them not emblematic figures but genuine and irreducible traces of Japan.

MARIKO SHIMIZU

I hardly knew her. She appeared in my seminars at Seijo University, she disappeared at the end. In between, she wrote me crowded, gnomic letters—about Saul Kripke, Heidegger, Wittgenstein, about Kundera, Stein, and Magritte, about *The Book of Tea, Hiroshima, Mon Amour, Beloved*. She always signed herself in Japanese, but I came to recognize her kanji.

In a certain slant of light, she could appear witchlike, a face lined prematurely, glimmering black eyes. Untypically for a Japanese, she cracked up at a joke before it was finished. Her letters, untypically too, were exercises in wit, weird associations, unflinching spirituality. She it was who explained to me, in postcards covered with a distinct, minuscule hand, the concepts of *wabi, sabi, shibui, isagiyoshi* (the samurai's aesthetic of sudden death). In other letters, she speculated about Cage, and the occult relations between *Music, Mushrooms,* and *Mu* (the void). Curiously, she also inquired about Cage's parents—who else inquires about them?

However esoteric, though, her missives were maniacally logical, playful at the same time, like certain kinds of music. They always struck a theme, a profoundly Japanese theme, clearly audible among all the overtones of Occidental learning. Yet she spurned myths of Japanese purity, a superior race. To her, vanity, in a neighbor or a rock star, was indescribably ugly, the ethical and the aesthetic commingling in her head as they so often do in Japanese art.

I barely knew Shimizu-san. I think her life was hard. I sensed in her a seriousness and a clownishness of mind akin to Zen. Where, then, had all her secret bitterness gone? Drained, I imagine, by the old sagacity, into the historic earth, into the immemorial sea, of Japan.

Mariko Shimizu knew but did not inhabit the past. Nor did I.

AMOR LOCI?

Over the years, Sally and I walked through many Japanese cities, drank a cup of coffee in many a *kissaten*. We would walk in various quarters and see the past spill itself before our eyes, vanishing into the ineluctable present—in Kyoto, a female motorcycle gang, thigh-booted and heavy-metaled, growling greetings to passersby; in Toyoma, a laser-cut building, standing on edge, a flying wedge of glass and sky. With the lovely, thick taste of Jamaican Blue Mountain coffee in our mouths, we felt a new, urban reality seep through our pores.

But pores are skin deep. Something else there beside people I knew, friends I have not all named, sinks slowly into the heart. How shall I put it?

In the MOA Museum in Atami, a black, lacquer calligraphy box: full moon, some golden reeds, a man, alone, sitting on a water buffalo, piping a tune through the silver hole in the sky, white shadows on the marsh, blackness all around. What more is there to say about our sublunary fate, except to remark on the patience of the buffalo?

Or a flower arrangement sent by a poet to our hotel room: following its original harmony of colors and shapes—I scarcely recognized a flower there—the arrangement subtly metamorphosed, passing through several lives, some petals wilting, others coming into bloom, a leaf shriveling, another sprouting, the whole seeming to preserve its essential form even as it finally withered into dry, crooked twigs in a bowl. Did poet or florist know that hands could summon all the seasons into a closed city room?

Or a performance by Ushio Amagatsu's Sankai Juku dancers: bodies wearing the rags of generations, ashes of death, moving as in a slow, apocalyptic dream, the formalism of anguish itself, life as inextinguishable breath, mouths torn open, eyes, fingers, legs, toes, torsos working, twisting, wringing the lineaments of existence from the void, no, from the bowels of the earth, the silence of the sea on the stage, a mountain on each dancer's back. (Sankai Juku: the Workshop of Mountain and Sea.) Even when the dancers return to us from their no-time, no-space, bowing to the audience with just a hint of the grotesque, their inhuman elegance can put a prima ballerina to shame.

These are stray moments, moments among many moments, that I have cherished to remind myself of what draws me, repeatedly, to Japan. Mere aestheticism, you say? Mere? Besides, beauty there often sweats like a dancer, inhales the human and exhales metaphysics. It may be the best part of the Japanese genius.

Still, I could not say, as John David Morley said in *Pictures from the Water Trade*, taking his cue perhaps from Chaplin, that I came to Japan because I saw an actor walk across a stage. I saw actors and dancers long after, the blind beggars of Hisashi Inoue's *The Great Doctor Yabuhara* stumbling brilliantly on the set, Ushio Amagatsu or Kuniko Kisanuki, kneading the earth slowly, slowly, with their bleached feet (*buto*: dancing, stomping on the ground). But Morley wisely left Japan when he found that he had become an alien to himself, a gaijin in his own eyes. I never lived there long enough for radical self-change.

Many years later, Morley wrote me a remarkable letter, from which I excerpt:

> I have no theory to propose here, only my own predilections. The location Japan, for instance, was only apparently the story of a journey from west to east in "Water Trade." Behind the "whim" of the actor crossing the stage is *a recognition of something instantly familiar*. And this feeling is conditioned by the Malay, Indonesian and Chinese nurses who looked after me as a small child in Singapore. The spiritual locus, then, is the place of belonging, which in my case is the place of origin but need not necessarily be so. In some sense the *spirit has stayed put here*, and the wanderings of the body are its avatars, and in my experience this is quest, the return to a centre of original stillness. For I have known people who had no prior links with the place to which they had to move to find this kind of correspondence of within and without. I have known people who *intuited* this place. For me the journey is a paradigm of movement back towards an origin, the *amor loci* that is (or holds out the promise of being) a sense of belonging. For me, that kind of journey could only be made once.
>
> Since getting back from Japan in 1976 I have become interested in the centripetal journeys, perhaps because the locus of the quest has been identified.

Amor loci. It was not of Japan, not of Egypt—was it still of my elective homeland, slapdash superpower, once the republic of my dreams? The words of Hugo of St. Victor come back to me: the perfect man has extinguished his *amor loci*. But I stand far from perfection, which I glimpsed in Japan, glimpsed only for as long as cherry blossoms quiver in the wind or fireflies flash in the universe's drifting light.

Some days, I think I have learned little from Japan, that I know little about it and want to know little more. Let Japan now discover its own identity, if "identity" it wants. Let it find there a myth, idea, or role to give it a place in the world, if it can find there a "there." I am done.

But most days, I know that in Japan I have sought and found—no, stumbled on—part of my aspiring self. *Lessness, leanness, dispossession*—these words sound a touch grand. Shall we say simplicity? Ah, but it is strange simplicity, made subtle by selflessness, made rigorous by contingency—that is, death. John Cage understood that simplicity well. May he and his "sunny disposition" rest in peace.

In a sense, then, my vacillations about Japan have never ceased. That is why I plan one more visit, board yet another plane. But I know that each journey can only confront me more sharply with my own, not Japan's, lacks. That is well: we grow through the cracks in our being, our lacks.

Between the Eagle and the Sun? In legend only, the eagle stares directly at the sun. It is otherwise in the world: we stare through distractions of the day, words lyrical or critical, clouds leavened by our longing. Yet we stare and stare.

About the Author

Ihab Hassan is Vilas Research Professor of English and Comparative Literature at the University of Wisconsin in Milwaukee. He has lectured widely in America, Australia, Africa, Asia, and Europe. The author of 12 books, 2 edited collections, and more than 150 articles, Hassan considers himself mainly an independent critic. Many of his works have been translated into Japanese.